Selfish, Jealous, Shortsighted, Stubborn, and Ungrateful

...And the Way Forward

I0142261

For Sue Meyer, who left us too soon

ISBN 979-8-9928066-1-8

"Let us beset the just one, because he is obnoxious to us;

he sets himself against our doings,

reproaches us for transgressions of the law,

and charges us with violations of our training."

- *Wisdom 2:12*

"This is why everyone hates moral philosophy professors."

- *The Good Place*[1]

---

[1] Schur, Michael, *The Good Place*, Season 1 Episode 7, Season 2 Episode 5, Season 2 Episode 11, etc., aired 2016-2020, NBC.

To the reader

This is a book about human nature, and the difficulty of getting humans to do the right thing.

Who is this book meant for?

It's meant for those charged with governance, including board members, senior leaders, compliance officers, and regulators.

It's meant for voters, the politicians they elect, and the administrators employed to do their will.

It's meant for anyone developing a new technology, process, or tool, who wants to think about the ethical and practical implications of how people will use it.

It's meant for anyone who's ever wondered, "Why did this other person just do that awful thing?"

It's meant for anyone who's ever looked in the mirror and wondered, "Why did I just do that awful thing?"

In short, I think it's meant for pretty much everyone.

I have a high degree of confidence in my observations about human nature. Their sources are timeless, and I see their truth reflected over and over again in my job, in the news, and in my daily interactions. I also provide thoughts about ways to mitigate the inherent obnoxiousness of human behavior in organizational settings. I have lower confidence in those recommendations. As G.K. Chesterton said, "While the reformer is always right about what is wrong, he is generally wrong about what is right."[2]

That doesn't mean we shouldn't try.

---

[2] Chesterton, G.K., "The Revolutions of the Young," *The Illustrated London News*, October 28, 1922, reprinted in *The Collected Works of G.K. Chesterton XXXII* (Ignatius Press, 1989). I've rendered the citation the way it's usually quoted, although in the original "the reformer" is simply "he."

About the author

I worked as an auditor in the U.S. and Latin America for eight years. I then spent sixteen years leading financial due diligence and strategy projects in the U.S. and internationally. Finally, I led four different quality and risk management organizations over the course of twelve years, managing hundreds of compliance professionals and overseeing tens of thousands of people. (Some of those roles overlapped – I'm not quite as old as adding up the numbers would suggest.)

I volunteer with the Missionaries of Charity. I teach catechism and serve as a bilingual lector and eucharistic minister.

I don't bring up my biography to convince you that I'm a particularly saintly person – I'm not. The reason is threefold:

(1) I believe my experience has given me a pretty good idea of human behavior in various settings.

(2) I found a surprising amount of overlap between the disciplines of catechism and risk assessment. Whether you think of the Bible as divine revelation or human literature, the best-selling book of all time[3] has some interesting things to say about very practical matters.

(3) I will throughout the book give examples of my own selfishness, jealousy, shortsightedness, stubbornness, and ingratitude. While I don't think I'm a particularly saintly person, I also don't think I'm a particularly awful one. I suspect things that are true of me are true of many others.

---

[3] "List of bestselling books," Wikimedia Foundation, last modified January 15, 2025, **https://en.wikipedia.org/wiki/List_of_best-selling_books**. At around 5 billion copies sold and distributed, the Bible beats the *Harry Potter* series by almost ten to one (which considering how much longer the Bible has been around, is a heck of a testament to J.K. Rowling as an author).

This is not a book about religion, or public accounting – although it will incorporate examples from both. Rather, it is meant to provide a broad framework to consider human behavior in a wide variety of organizational contexts. Hopefully readers will consider my behavior and that of others I describe, ponder their own and what they experience around them, and see some general truths reflected. Ideally, they will come up with their own thoughts on pragmatic approaches to dealing with those truths.

Introduction

Wouldn't it be great if everyone just did the right thing, whatever that was? Failing that, wouldn't it be great if only bad people did bad things? It would certainly make society easier to organize. But that's not how humans are.

Human flaws are almost too numerous to count, and everyone has their own way of cataloging them. The Catholic Church has the seven deadly sins. The moral philosopher Judith Shklar focused instead on the "ordinary vices" of cruelty, hypocrisy, snobbery, betrayal, and misanthropy.[4] Organizational behaviorists like Max Bazerman[5] and Jason Brennan tend to focus on moral blindspots, conformism, weakness of will, and bad incentives. For example, my son encountered a class taught by Brennan at Georgetown University called "Managing jerks, assholes, & freeloaders"[6] (subsequently changed to "Managing flawed people" for fairly obvious reasons). I have my own thoughts after thirty years of auditing, due diligence, and running compliance organizations.

When I teach catechism, I start with the Old Testament. I tell my students that you can learn pretty much everything you need to know about human nature from the first two books of the Bible, Genesis and Exodus. Specifically, people are selfish, jealous, shortsighted, stubborn, and ungrateful. That is almost universally true. As Dan Ariely wrote in one of my favorite books, *The Honest Truth About Dishonesty*, very few individuals are saints or sociopaths – most fall into the common run of humanity, subject to normal human frailty.[7]

---

[4] Shklar, Judith, *Ordinary Vices* (The Belknap Press of Harvard University Press, 1984), "Thinking About Vices."

[5] See, for example, Bazerman, Max, and Ann Tenbrunsel, *Blind Spots* (Princeton University Press, 2011), "The Gap between Intended and Actual Ethical Behavior."

[6] Dr. Jason Brennan, Robert J. and Elizabeth Flanagan Family Professor of Strategy, Economics, Ethics, and Public Policy at the McDonough School of Business at Georgetown University.

[7] Ariely, Dan, *The Honest Truth About Dishonesty* (HarperCollins Publishers, 2012), "Fun with the Fudge Factor."

Ariely is alleged to have spectacularly proven his own point by using false data in his research about falsification. Francesca Gino, a Harvard professor and frequent collaborator of Ariely's and Bazerman's, is accused of the same thing. I don't know the detailed facts of those cases and don't presume to judge the scholars in question.[8] I am a huge fan of Dan Ariely's work, I handed out copies of *The Honest Truth About Dishonesty* to my colleagues in compliance functions, and I will quote his thinking throughout this book. I very nearly contracted Francesca Gino to help me with a compliance problem. I bring up the accusations not to indict these scholars, but to suggest that the authors of the Bible knew certain universal truths about humanity that can be applied to everyone, even the scholarly community of ethicists.[9] We ignore those truths at our peril.

That doesn't mean we should simply surrender to our own worst instincts. There is tremendous value in trust. When I lived in Chile in the 1990s, the country's retail process looked like it had been designed by auditors:

- To buy a deodorant stick at the pharmacy, you asked a clerk for it.
- He gave you a form in triplicate.
- You took the form to a second clerk at the cash register and paid.
- He stamped the form, gave you two copies, and kept one.
- Then finally you took the two stamped copies to a third clerk.
- He stamped the form again, kept a copy, and gave you the deodorant and the last copy.

---

[8] Perhaps even more ironically, the researchers who questioned Ariely and Gino's work recently retracted their own paper on bad research methodology because of… wait for it… bad research methodology. Subbaraman, Nidhi, "These Researchers Critique Bad Science. Now Their Own Paper Has Been Retracted," *The Wall Street Journal,* October 30, 2024.

[9] Indeed, a study by Eric Schwitzgebel found that ethics professors appeared to be more likely than other philosophy professors to steal textbooks (Schwitzgebel, Eric, "Do Ethicists Steal More Books," *Philosophical Psychology 22:6,* 2009).

Compare the number of people and the amount of time involved to simply getting the deodorant off the shelf and scanning it through a self-checkout machine. No one wants to live in the kind of low-trust system that existed in Chile back then – it's wasteful and inefficient. It is critically important to build systems and processes that enhance trust. That is why, for example, CPAs are required to "accept the obligation to act in a way that will serve the public interest, honor the public trust, and demonstrate a commitment to professionalism."[10] And it's why the Securities and Exchange Commission highlights auditors' and other gatekeepers' "responsibility to the public interest and to act ethically and with integrity in every professional activity."[11] Institutions that build trust are critical to a well-ordered society. They let us enter into a wide range of transactions – from buying deodorant to buying stocks – without believing we're going to be ripped off. There's a reason Dante consigns fraudsters to the eighth circle of hell.[12]

But when we think about governance and compliance, we should keep the truths of human nature in mind. I am frequently selfish, jealous, shortsighted, stubborn, and ungrateful. I suspect that most leaders are as well. So are the people they lead. And so are the accomplished, well-meaning individuals who are chosen to oversee compliance functions. Even the regulators set up as the ultimate watchers are subject to the same human frailties. So when we design institutions to ensure that people "do the right thing," it helps to keep human nature firmly at the forefront of our minds.

---

[10] AICPA Code of Professional Conduct Section 0.300.030.01, American Institute of CPAs, effective December 15, 2014, updated through December 2023.

[11] Munter, Paul, SEC Chief Accountant, Statement on June 8, 2022, "The Critical Importance of the General Standard of Auditor Independence and an Ethical Culture for the Accounting Profession," **https://www.sec.gov/newsroom/speeches-statements/munter-20220608**.

[12] Alighieri, Dante, *The Divine Comedy*, trans. Gerald J. Davis (Insignia Publishing, 2021), original text c.1321, "Inferno."

The goal of this book is twofold. First, to demonstrate the ways in which people – not just "bad people," but people in general – are very often selfish, jealous, shortsighted, stubborn, and ungrateful. And second, to provide thoughts on how the governance of businesses and other social organizations can be designed around those characteristics. I'll draw on three decades of experience as an auditor, a due diligence specialist, and a leader of compliance teams, combined with bits and pieces of theology, economics, psychology, sociology, and moral philosophy. But hopefully more than anything else, the experiences and recommendations will resonate with readers who honestly reflect on what each of us has observed about human nature.

For example, in all of my roles – auditor, due diligence specialist, compliance team leader – I rarely found people who were actively telling me bald-faced lies. Sure, it happened. I was once sitting three feet away from the CEO of a Latin American cable company, I asked him a direct question about disputes with his vendors, and he lied to my face. Out of almost 400,000 people in the firm I worked for, my team would occasionally find people who were deliberately doing the wrong thing and knowingly concealing it. But those were very rare, and it was noncontroversial to simply fire them after a thorough investigation. More typical – and in fact almost ubiquitous – were the people who were just doing what was easiest to get the job done and cover their backs. The controller at the audit client who gave me the first answer that came into his head to get me to go away faster. The nepotism I found when I performed diligence on family-owned businesses. The people – too many to count – who were narrowly focused on what was best for them personally, not for the organization.

Some of these points may seem obvious to people who have, well, been around people. But I believe it's important to clearly establish the premises both in the realm of moral philosophy and organizational design. Contractarian philosophers like John Rawls tend to leave out the unfortunate sides of human nature when they develop moral theories.[13] To me, that's a bit like the assumption in high school physics that every object is a steel sphere operating in a frictionless vacuum – intellectually interesting, and simpler to deal with in theory, but not very useful for practical engineering. Similarly, a lot of economists assume that humans are as rational as the average Vulcan from Star Trek – again, good for making your mathematical models work, but not a great representation of the real world.

In reality, humans are animals with genetic wiring that pulls our strings to get us to behave in certain ways, and those behaviors can be quite obnoxious – both to those around us and sometimes even to ourselves. As Robert Wright notes in *The Moral Animal*, "I don't think I'm spoiling the end of the movie by noting here that the puppeteer seems to have exactly zero regard for the happiness of the puppets."[14] The evolutionary imperatives that drive our behavior were historically very good at passing along our genes – by definition. They're not necessarily great at making us good or happy people. We should aspire to better, as Steven Pinker suggests when he notes that "the ultimate goal of natural selection is to propagate genes, but that does not mean that the ultimate goal of people is to propagate genes."[15]

---

[13] One topic I'm not going to touch are the relative merits of Hobbes' view that humans are inherently corrupt and only tamed by society, versus Rousseau's view that humans are inherently good and corrupted by society. I'm going to take it as a given that 99.9% of readers carry smartphones, use antibiotics, and generally participate in an organized society. So the question of whether we would all be devils or saints in the absence of that society is irrelevant, although I tend to agree with St. Augustine that "the only innocent feature in babies is the weakness of their frames; the minds of infants are far from innocent." (St. Augustine, *The Confessions*, trans. Maria Boulding, O.S.B., (New City Press, 1997), original text c.400). I also don't intend to address the many complex cases where there are competing duties and it's hard to decide what the "right" answer is. This book is focused on cases where most people would agree on the right thing to do, and people just don't do it.
[14] Wright, Robert, *The Moral Animal* (Vintage Books, 1994), "Male and Female."
[15] Pinker, Steven, *How the Mind Works* (W.W. Norton & Company, 1997), "Standard Equipment."

Maybe, as I heard suggested on a podcast I recently watched, the very smart people in the tech sector will finally help us solve these moral quandaries. Maybe. Perhaps in much the same way the very smart people in the financial sector helped us eliminate all risk from the financial system right around, say, 2008. Or, you know, maybe not.

Slightly over a decade ago I converted to Catholicism. Looking at it from the outside, I could easily understand the criticisms leveled against the religion by non-Catholics. It seems to suffer from a moral code that is at once too strict and too lax. Everyone is always sinning, and yet even the gravest sin can be wiped away by confession and repentance. There's something about that pairing of ideas that offends common sense. Shouldn't we have a more achievable model of acceptable behavior, and rigorously punish transgressions against it? But I've come to believe that the Catholic approach is not only theologically sound, but provides a good practical basis for modeling human action. There's something very true about Saint Paul's Letter to the Romans where he writes:

> I do not understand what I do. For what I want to do I do not do, but what I hate I do. For I have the desire to do what is good, but I cannot carry it out. For I do not do the good I want to do, but the evil I do not want to do—this I keep on doing.[16]

In the following chapters, we'll explore why Paul, whom Christians regard as one of the greatest saints, may have struggled with doing the right thing.

---

[16] Romans 7:15, 18-19.

I. Selfish

"Egoism is a perversity as old as the world
and is scarcely peculiar to one form of
society more than another."

- Alexis De Tocqueville[17]

In my catechism class I teach the story of Adam and Eve as allegory.[18] The third chapter of Genesis tells us all sorts of interesting things about humans. One of my favorites is how Genesis 3:12 manages to pack both buck-passing and victim-blaming (if God can be considered a victim) into one line from Adam: "The woman whom you put here with me – she gave me fruit from the tree, so I ate it." In other words, "It wasn't my fault, it was my wife's," and also, "By the way, God, you're the one who put her here, so it's really your fault."

But to me, the core lesson is in Genesis 3:5: "You will be like gods."

Our allegorical Adam and Eve lived in a perfect world, where all their needs were provided for. But it wasn't enough – they wanted to be gods as well. They had one job – not eating from the tree that God had forbidden to them. They blew it because everything had to be all about them. They would accept no limits on their actions. Within days of when I began to write this book, the Catholic Church issued its Declaration of *Infinite Dignity* in which it reminded readers of "the age-old temptation to make oneself God."[19]

[17] De Tocqueville, Alexis, *Democracy in America Vol.2,* trans. Gerald E. Bevan (Penguin Books, 2003), original text 1840, "Individualism in Democratic Countries."

[18] Allegorical interpretation of the Bible has an ancient and distinguished history. See for example St. Augustine's allegorical interpretations of Genesis in *The Confessions* or Surah Al-Imran 7 of the Quran (translation by Marmaduke Pickthall, Safa-Scripts, 2024). For a particularly good recent analysis of allegory in Genesis, see Pope Benedict XVI (Cardinal Joseph Ratzinger at the time of writing), *In the Beginning...*, trans. Boniface Ramsey, O.P. (William B. Eerdmans Publishing Co., 1995), original text 1986.

[19] Declaration of the Dicastery for the Doctrine of the Faith "Dignitas Infinita" on Human Dignity, April 8, 2024,
https://press.vatican.va/content/salastampa/en/bollettino/pubblico/2024/04/08/240408c.html.

Maybe that doesn't resonate with you. If you don't think you're particularly selfish (and most of us don't think so), try reciting – and truly meaning – the Litany of Humility. It says, in summarized part:

> *Deliver me from the desire of being praised, preferred to others, approved... Deliver me from the fear of being humiliated, despised, forgotten... Grant me the grace to desire to be set aside, to go unnoticed, that others may be preferred to me in everything.*[20]

I try to pray the Litany of Humility sincerely. It's very, very hard to mean it. Try to feel good about it the next time you're unjustly passed over for a promotion, or your opinion is ignored, or someone badmouths you. Try not to be angry at those responsible. When I mentioned that to my wife, her reaction was, "You're not ready for it." Which made me mad, because she was saying I wasn't humble enough for the Litany of Humility. The fact that she said that wounded my pride – which proved her point.

You can find the Litany of Humility at:

https://www.ewtn.com/catholicism/devotions/litany-of-humility-245

Try it. If you're not Christian, you can remove the references to Jesus without significantly changing the meaning. Or if you prefer, you can try the remarkably similar *Eight Verses on the Training of the Mind* from Tibetan Buddhism.[21] See if you can say them, and mean them.

Selfishness has been around as long as humanity. If you don't want to take the Bible's word for it, try Thucydides in the *History of the Peloponnesian War:* "The strong do what they will and the weak suffer what they must."[22]

---

[20] Rafael Cardinal Merry del Val y Zulueta, **https://www.ewtn.com/catholicism/devotions/litany-of-humility-245**.

[21] **https://www.dalailama.com/teachings/training-the-mind**.

[22] Thucydides, *History of the Peloponnesian War*, trans. Richard Crawley, 1874 (Red Skull Publishing, 2017), original text c.400 BC.

Think we've outgrown it? Consider that a couple of thousand years later, Friedrich Nietzsche, who famously declared that "God is dead," enshrined the "will to power"[23] as the sole driving force in human endeavor. The philosopher Bertrand Russell characterized Nietzsche as insecure and megalomaniacal... but admitted that his philosophy was "internally self-consistent" and struggled to refute it.[24]

Alan Bloom wrapped it up pretty well:

> *What begins in a search if not precisely for selfish pleasure... then at least for the avoidance of and release from suffering and distress, transmogrified into a life-style and a right, becomes the ground of moral superiority. The comfortable, unconstrained life is morality.... Self-serving is expressed as, and really believed to be, disinterested principle....*[25]

Bloom isn't saying that we're "selfish" in the sense of stepping on others to get ahead, or stealing from widows and orphans. But he is saying that we're selfish in the sense that our primary preoccupation is with what we want. We may support some higher cause or another, but most of us do that from well within our personal comfort zone. Or as Tocqueville says, "In democratic societies, every citizen is habitually busy considering one very small subject, namely himself."[26]

---

[23] Nietzsche, Friedrich, *Thus Spoke Zarathustra*, trans. Thomas Common (William A. Chapko, 2010), original text 1883.
[24] Russell, Bertrand, *The History of Western Philosophy* (Sinon & Schuster, 1945), "Friedrich Nietzsche."
[25] Bloom, Allan, *The Closing of the American Mind* (Simon & Schuster, 1987), "Values."
[26] De Tocqueville, *Democracy in America,* "Why American Writers and Speakers Are Often Bombastic".

Even Karl Marx was a big believer in selfishness, and not just of the ruling class, possessed of the "selfish misconception that induces you to transform into eternal laws of nature and of reason, the social forms springing from your present mode of production and form of property."[27] He also extended it to "the social scum, that passively rotting mass thrown off by the lowest layers of old society... part of a bribed tool of reactionary intrigue."[28] The top and bottom of Marx's social scale are both selfish. Even the proletariat acts only in its own interests, the "conquest of political power," because "man's consciousness changes with every change in the conditions of his material existence, in his social relations and in his social life."[29]

Saul Alinsky phrased it more succinctly than Marx:

> *Political realists see the world as it is: an arena of power politics moved primarily by perceived immediate self-interests, where morality is rhetorical rationale for expedient action and self-interest.*[30]

Various moral philosophies, both religious and secular, attempt to limit human selfishness. The Judeo-Christian and Greco-Roman traditions have stated that "freedom" means not just freedom from the tyranny of others, but perhaps more importantly freedom from the tyranny of oneself – that is, the tyranny of one's base, selfish desires.

Buddhism, Taoism, and other spiritual practices cultivate a similar concept of detachment. They observe that beyond a fairly low level of material well-being, what philosophers call the "good life" is much more dependent on our own mental outlook than worldly success. The Dalai Lama noted that:

---

[27] Marx, Karl and Friedrich Engels, *The Communist Manifesto*, 1848, "Proletarians and Communists."
[28] Ibid, "Bourgeois and Proletarians."
[29] Ibid, "Proletarians and Communists."
[30] Alinsky, Saul, *Rules for Radicals* (Vintage Books, 1971), "The Purpose."

Success may result in a temporary feeling of elation, or tragedy may send us into a period of depression, but sooner or later our overall level of happiness tends to migrate back to a certain baseline.... As long as there is a lack of the inner discipline that brings calmness of mind, no matter what external facilities or conditions you have, they will never give you the feeling of joy and happiness that you are seeking[31]... When I speak of discipline, I'm referring to self-discipline, not discipline that's externally imposed on you by someone else.[32]

"Self-government" therefore has a dual meaning – before people could govern themselves in a democracy, they had to govern their own passions. Patrick Deneen wrote:

Liberty had long been believed to be the condition of self-rule that forestalled tyranny, within both the polity and the individual soul. Liberty was thus thought to involve discipline and training in self-limitation of desires, and corresponding social and political arrangements that sought to inculcate corresponding virtues that fostered the arts of self-government.[33]

Those efforts are noble and essential. Everyone should follow their moral traditions that mitigate selfishness. But let's also be realistic. Jesus of Nazareth was betrayed by one of his twelve apostles for money. Another apostle, Saint Peter, "the rock on whom Jesus would build his Church," swore that he would die for Jesus and within a few hours had denied him three times to save his own skin.[34]   I think it's fair to say that selfishness will always be with us.

~~~

---

[31] HH Dalai Lama and Howard C. Cutler, MD, *The Art of Happiness* (Riverhead Books, 1998), "The Sources of Happiness."

[32] Ibid, "Training the Mind for Happiness."

[33] Deneen, Patrick, *Why Liberalism Failed* (Yale University Press, 2018), "Unsustainable Liberalism." For those not familiar with Deneen, it may be important to clarify that he doesn't mean "liberalism" as just the views of Democrats or "left liberals"; he also considers most Republicans to be "classical liberals" or "right liberals" falling under his definition of liberalism.

[34] Pick your Gospel of choice for both Judas and Peter. The stories are remarkably similar across all four.

If people are going to serve their self-interest, what does that mean for designing an organization that does the right thing? Jesus advised his disciples that they should "be shrewd as serpents and simple as doves"[35] – that while they should do the right thing, they should be aware that other people (and indeed they themselves) might not do so, even when they say they will.

Let's consider a values statement:

> RESPECT: We treat others as we would like to be treated ourselves. We do not tolerate abusive or disrespectful treatment. Ruthlessness, callousness, and arrogance don't belong here.
>
> INTEGRITY: We work with customers and prospects openly, honestly, and sincerely. When we say we will do something, we will do it; when we say we cannot or will not do something, then we won't do it.

Those statements were taken from Enron's 1998 Annual Report.[36]

---

[35] Matthew 10:16.
[36] McLean, Bethany and Peter Elkind, *The Smartest Guys in the Room* (Penguin Group, 2003), "Our Values."

I never audited Enron, but I was working as an auditor in Texas when they went under. My audit client took their number seven spot on the Fortune 500. A couple of years earlier, I had been asked to research how Enron's broadband trading platform worked. I spent a few days on it and couldn't for the life of me figure out how to trade broadband derivatives – long-haul fiber routes just weren't liquid enough. I told the partner in charge that if it was possible to do it, I wasn't smart enough to figure out how.[37] As it turns out, Enron couldn't figure out how to do it either. And then I spent a fair amount of the early 2000s cleaning up after the Arthur Andersen elephant at Global Crossing, Qwest, and Worldcom, two of which became clients of mine and the other the subject of one of my more intense due diligence analyses.

When I had graduated from college a decade before, Andersen had been the Marine Corps of public accounting.[38] If you wanted to work really hard and learn how to do a good audit, you went to Andersen.[39] An FBI agent at a recruiting event back then said to me, "It's not just that Andersen guys all wear black shoes – it's that they all wear the same brand of black shoes." When the FBI thinks you're too conformist, that says something.

---

[37] I received an invaluable lesson on understanding complexity on one of my first audits, which was a water utility in Chile. I was sent to ask the corporate controller about a change in an account balance. I got an explanation but when I started to write it down, it no longer made sense to me. As I was sitting around staring at the ceiling, my senior came by and asked me what I was doing. I said, "Thinking." He sarcastically asked, "What's the charge code for that?" I explained what had happened, and he told me to go back and ask the controller again. Since Spanish was my second language, I was new, and I didn't know Chilean GAAP very well, I suggested he go instead rather than have me annoy the controller by asking again. He asked, "Are you stupid?" I replied that I hadn't thought so until about five minutes ago, but was now willing to entertain the possibility. He told me that I wasn't stupid, and that corporate controllers always tell the new audit staff the first thing that comes into their heads to make us go away. It's not that they're trying to cover something up – it's that they don't want to be bothered with us. He told me to keep asking the question until I got an answer that made sense. It was excellent advice, and things might have gone differently at Enron if the Andersen audit partner had followed it.

[38] That phrasing was commonplace during the early 1990s and was used by Andersen partners themselves, for example Rich Lowe as cited by Barbara Toffler in *Final Accounting* (Broadway Books, 2003), "The Andersen Way."

[39] I didn't. I worked for two of the other Big Six (later Big Four) public accounting firms instead. I still learned how to do a good audit.

So the collapse of Enron and Andersen intrigued me. Andersen was one of the world's most respected public accounting firms. From its founding in 1913 into the 1970s, Andersen had been the conscience of the profession, on multiple occasions resigning from significant audits when it felt the clients used accounting methods that were technically permissible but misleading.[40] Its fall had been a tragedy that would have its eponymous founder rolling in his grave. And Enron wasn't just a scam like Bernie Madoff's pyramid scheme. Something had gone badly wrong with a large group of people who couldn't be simply dismissed as crooks or sociopaths. As McLean and Elkin noted:

> *In the public eye, Enron's mission was nothing more than the cover story for a massive fraud. But what brought Enron down was something more complex – and more tragic – than simple thievery. The tale of Enron is a story of human weakness, of hubris and greed and rampant self-delusion; of ambition run amok...[41]*

Furthermore, the perpetrators didn't seem like a collection of criminals. They were intellectuals, children of preachers, veterans. Lots of veterans. That part was interesting to me. I would have thought that those who had served in the military would have been indoctrinated with ideals of honor, service, and self-sacrifice. Then I thought back to a conversation I'd had in the 1990s with a colleague who had served as a Marine supply sergeant during Operation Desert Storm. He explained the incredible operational difference between peacetime and wartime service. As he described it, in peacetime, if a Marine wanted an extra magazine for his assault rifle, you asked him to come back with a requisition form in triplicate, signed by the colonel commanding the base (similar to buying deodorant in Chile, but even more bureaucratic). If that same Marine ran up during the war and wanted a main battle tank, you handed him the keys[42] and told him where it was parked. My colleague drew a simple distinction between real rules and fake rules – you followed the real rules because if you didn't, someone died. The fake rules were only followed if they didn't conflict with the real rules.

---

[40] Toffler, *Final Accounting*, "The Making of an Android."

[41] McLean and Elkind, *The Smartest Guys in the Room*, Introduction.

[42] I'm told that while tanks do not have ignition keys, the command compartment is locked.

I think military personnel are very good at figuring out the distinction between real and fake rules because the stakes are so high. The veterans at Enron then applied those lessons to their new employer:

- Real rule: Make your revenue and profit forecasts.

- Fake rule: All the stuff in the values statement.

The stakes obviously weren't life-or-death at Enron, but the principle was the same. If you followed the real rules, you were promoted and financially rewarded. And you could get away with ignoring the fake rules, especially if they conflicted with the real rules.

In much of the modern world, the real rules tend to be about money. As the French philosopher, activist, and mystic Simone Weil said, "Bourgeois society is infected by monomania; the monomania of accounting."[43]

Money has obvious advantages as a metric and a motivator. It's easy to quantify. It's fungible, so it can be used for anything – food, shelter, healthcare, college tuition, charitable donations. But that fungibility comes with complete moral neutrality. A dollar doesn't know or care if you earned revenue from inventing a life-saving vaccine or selling arms to a warlord. It doesn't know or care if your bonus is based on selling a product that everyone wants or cooking the books. It doesn't know or care if you're going to donate it to Doctors Without Borders or buy yourself a gold-plated toilet seat. So its very fungibility and neutrality can make it a dangerous metric and motivator. As Michael Sandel puts it:

> *In its own way, market reasoning also empties public life of moral argument. Part of the appeal of markets is that they don't pass judgment on the preferences they satisfy.*[44]

I am not suggesting (nor does Sandel) that companies do away with double entry bookkeeping, or try to reward their employees with praise alone. A pat on the head and the feeling of having done the right thing don't pay the rent, and human beings have legitimate expenses and aspirations.

---

[43] Weil, Simone, *Memorable Quotations*, compiled and edited by Carol A. Dingle (2012), originally appearing in "La Rationalisation," 1937.
[44] Sandel, Michael, *What Money Can't Buy* (Farrar, Strauss and Giroux, 2012), "Introduction: Markets and Morals."

But neither is it a good idea to focus exclusively on making the numbers as a measure of success – either for a company or for an individual.

Over two decades ago, before Enron went under, the senior partner on a new audit told me and the team to "do a 'C' audit." We weren't quite sure what that meant, but we assumed it meant to do the bare minimum, because our budget was low and we couldn't do an "A" audit and achieve profitability on the engagement. As it happened, we didn't know how to do a "C" audit so we did everything we thought we needed to do. And as it also happened, the client was a former Andersen client – which we picked up before Andersen imploded – and Andersen hadn't even been doing a "C" audit. Interestingly enough, the audit partner who told us to do a "C" audit was also a military veteran, who had perhaps also internalized that hitting the numbers was the real rule.

Years later (but still many years ago), when I made partner myself, money was still a big motivator. At the meeting where we were inducted into the partnership, we were presented with a challenge. What would keep us motivated to keep giving 110% now that we had already grasped the brass ring? I expected that perhaps there would be an appeal to the public interest, or the legacy of those who had gone before us, or our responsibility to those who would come after. Instead, the presenter put up a picture of a nice house (somewhat like mine) and commented, "This is a partner's house. With a little yardwork, it could clean up nicely." He then put up a picture of a mansion and continued, "This is a managing partner's house." The implication was perfectly clear – we would keep working hard because we wanted more money.[45]

And I have to admit I bought into that. As a young partner, I drove a Chrysler. As a senior partner, I was driving a Cadillac. I found myself looking forward to building a "dream house" on an acre and a half of land we had bought with a view of the Hudson River. Sure, I told myself that those things didn't really matter to me, as demonstrated by my donations of time and money to charity. Frankly, I was lying to myself.

---

[45] Despite the fact that all partners were already earning well above the $75,000 identified as the "saturation point" for happiness in the famous study conducted a few years later in 2010 by Daniel Kahneman and Angus Deaton, *High income improves evaluation of life but not emotional well-being*, **http://www.pnas.org/cgi/doi/10.1073/pnas.1011492107**. While subsequent studies have challenged the $75.000 figure, partner compensation at a Big Four firm is probably above whatever the "saturation point" is.

~~~

If you're still with me, we've established that people are selfish. And we've established that when people are selfish they tend to care about money, because it's an easy thing to care about. So what can we do about it?

I believe the first step is to simply understand that people are selfish and will serve their own self-interest. Most studies of governance and agency theory acknowledge that fact and try to mitigate the resulting harm by aligning incentives. And those incentives are usually monetary.

Again, there's nothing wrong with money *per se*. It's easy to measure, it's morally neutral, and it can be exchanged for all kinds of useful things. It's fungible – you don't have to know what motivates people because money can be traded for so many of the things that motivate them. So it's a very tempting measurement and incentive mechanism. But it can also miss the point. As Max Bazerman notes:

> *Reward systems are usually well intentioned, yet they tend to miss the mark because they fail to anticipate how employees will respond to them. They are simplistic, focusing on a single objective. By ignoring how employees will achieve outlined goals, they produce unintentional behavior, and they discourage desirable behaviors that aren't rewarded.*[46]

I suggest that the first question any organization needs to ask is "What really matters to us?"

Revenue and profitability should be an outcome of successfully executing on "what really matters to us." But because money is morally neutral, revenue and profitability should not be the drivers.

---

[46] Bazerman and Tenbrunsel, *Blind Spots*, "Placing False Hope in the 'Ethical Organization.'"

What really matters is hugely variable based on the product or service provided. For example, if you are making plastic toy soldiers, 90% reliability may be perfectly acceptable if it keeps costs down. Let's say it costs $5 to make a bag of a hundred toy soldiers where 90% of them are perfect and 10% have melted to the side or don't quite have their whole gun. And let's say it would cost $10 to make a bag that was 99% perfect. Most people would likely prefer the cheaper bag because they could buy two bags for $10, and have one hundred and eighty perfect toy soldiers, rather than buying one bag of the better made soldiers for the same $10 and only having ninety-nine perfect toy soldiers. But for obvious reasons, if you're making commercial aircraft, you'd better be aiming for better than 90% perfection, and better than 99% perfection, no matter how much it costs.

The public is usually pretty good at telling you what it wants. Back in the old wireline telecom days, telephone networks were designed with "five nines" of reliability – a call was expected to successfully go through 99.999% of the time. Modern cellular networks probably don't even achieve "two nines" of reliability – while I haven't measured it, I'm pretty sure calls complete successfully less than 99.0% of the time. As it turns out, that's fine with most users, because of the added convenience of being able to carry your phone with you anywhere and do all sorts of things with it that we didn't imagine in the landline era. It would be prohibitively expensive to achieve 99.999% cellular coverage. Cellular customers are looking for different things than five nines, like cost, data capacity, and portability.

Different entities in the same market may have very different value propositions. A Toyota Camry and a Ferrari 812 Superfast are both cars, but they are targeting very different consumers. The Toyota is supremely reliable and about as exciting as a refrigerator. The Ferrari is pure excitement on wheels – with maintenance costs to match. Staying true to your value proposition is generally a good thing because it keeps you close to what really matters. When Ford owned Jaguar, they turned the perfectly good Ford Mondeo into the perfectly good Jaguar X-Type. The problem was that customers didn't think a Ford was the proper basis for a Jaguar. Jaguar's brand suffered as a result.[47]

---

[47] See for example Turkus, Brandon, "Jaguar Design Boss Admits X-Type Was a Mistake," *Autoblog*, September 19, 2013. Out of personal loyalty to Cadillac, I consign to this footnote the even more pointed story of Cadillac turning the Chevy Cavalier into the not perfectly good Cadillac Cimarron.

The point is that you should measure, as closely as possible, whatever it is that you are actually trying to achieve. That is your mission – as a person or an organization. Emile Durkheim, the founder of the modern discipline of sociology,[48] divided the world into the profane (the mundane business of making a living for yourself) and the sacred (sentiments inspiring awe, devotion, or respect).[49] Most successful organizations have a mission, what they're trying to achieve, which is in a sense "sacred" to them. For Durkheim, the sacred was not necessarily supernaturally religious, but rather something that governed moral behavior in society. As has been abundantly noted, people today are searching for some sense of meaning, including in the workplace.[50] That meaning can often be achieved by focusing on the actual goal. In the words of the Vietnamese Buddhist monk Thich Nhat Hanh:

> *Each thought, each action in the sunlight of awareness is sacred. In this light, no boundary exists between the sacred and the profane.[51]*

To borrow a common phrase, the sense of the "sacred" or "mission" is a way to change people's mindset from "I" to "we." Jonathan Haidt calls this activating the 10% "bee-ish" (cooperative) element of human nature, to overcome the 90% "chimp-ish" (selfish) element.[52]

One of my favorite quotes from Nietzsche is, "The most basic form of human stupidity is forgetting what we are trying to accomplish."[53] In other words, forgetting the mission. Revenue and profitability might be acceptable proxies... or they might not. Or they might only be up to the point where something goes horribly wrong, because a focus on the measurable numbers of revenue and profitability overtook the focus on what really mattered, which was harder to measure.

---

[48] Setting aside Ibn Khaldun, whom I'll cite later, and who could make a good claim to be the first sociologist five hundred years before Durkheim.

[49] Durkheim, Emile, *The Elementary Forms of Religious Life*, trans. Joseph Ward Swain, 1912, Introduction.

[50] See for example Bindley, Katherine and Chip Cutter, "Young People Are Taking Over the Workplace, and That's a Problem for Bosses," *The Wall Street Journal*, September 2, 2024.

[51] Thich Nhat Hanh, *Peace Is Every Step* (Bantam Books, 1991), "Breathe! You are Alive."

[52] Haidt, Jonathan, *The Righteous Mind* (Pantheon Books, 2012), "The Hive Switch."

[53] At least, the quote is attributed to Nietzsche. I have a book of his aphorisms and couldn't find that anywhere, although he was very fond of the word "stupidity."

"Deciding what *not* to do is as important as deciding what to do."[54] So said Steve Jobs, and I agree that a sense of mission can be as much about limiting scope as expanding it. Many observers (and I) feel that the singular genius of Jobs at Apple was to focus on the simplified user experience of the product design. Sometimes that meant not doing something – for example, when Jobs regained leadership of Apple in 1997, he shrank the number of computer products from thousands to four. He also killed off Apple's business of selling its operating system to "clone" hardware manufacturers. In the near term, both moves clearly caused lost sales. In the long term, they protected the mission.

The mission can of course be defined too narrowly. Kodak famously stuck so doggedly to its expertise in making film that it went bankrupt when digital photography took over.[55] In my own profession, I firmly believe that there are many services outside of financial statement audit that are absolutely within the core competency of public accounting firms. But as Paul Munter of the SEC noted, those services need to be consistent with and "remain focused on the trusted role that public accountants play in the disclosure of high-quality financial information to the investing public."[56] Munter went on in a subsequent speech to emphasize that:

> *To be an effective public watchdog, audit-firm leadership must set the right tone at the top by always placing the public-interest obligations of our profession ahead of business interests and profits…. Technical excellence and integrity should be rewarded at least as much as billing, profitability, and business development.*[57]

---

[54] Isaacson, Walter, *Steve Jobs*, (Simon & Schuster, 2011), "Think Different: Jobs as iCEO."

[55] As is usually the case, this story is less one-sided than commonly presented. As described in Michael Hiltzik's article "Kodak's Long Fade to Black" in the *Los Angeles Times* (December 4, 2011), Kodak did in fact make significant investments in digital technology – just not significant enough.

[56] Munter, "The Critical Importance of the General Standard of Auditor Independence and an Ethical Culture for the Accounting Profession."

[57] Munter, Paul, SEC Chief Accountant, Statement on May 15, 2024, "Fostering a Healthy "Tone at the Top" at Audit Firms," **https://www.sec.gov/newsroom/speeches-statements/munter-statement-audit-firms-051524**

Let's hypothetically say that in a due diligence engagement a partner managed to commit a trifecta of quality errors. Say he crossed over from serving the seller to serving the buyer after the deal was signed, but before it closed, without getting the consent of his original client. Let's say he didn't reperform engagement acceptance to make sure the work was permissible for the new client under auditor independence rules. And let's say he was prepared to sign off on a report prepared by a team in another country, written in a language he didn't speak. Finally, let's say this partner had the highest revenue of anyone in his group. How do you think he did when annual evaluations were performed?

There's a real temptation to say that as long as no actual regulatory violation occurred and no one got sued, the missteps are just foot faults that aren't worth sanctioning. But if quality matters, is it wise to send the message that it's okay not to be good as long as you're lucky? I once scolded a practice leader for taking shortcuts on our processes. Because he was a skilled technician as well as a good revenue generator, he was deeply offended. He asked if I thought he wasn't doing good work. I explained that I knew his work was good because he had decades of experience and judgment, but my concern was that his staff, who didn't yet have that experience or judgment, were learning a lesson he didn't intend to teach – that the process didn't matter. To his credit, he conceded the point.

As Munter noted:

> *Less-experienced staff watch what their managers do. If they see their managers bend the rules or make exceptions for profitable partners who engage in inappropriate conduct, less-experienced staff may assume that this behavior is the path to rise through the ranks. This is why firm leadership must make ethics and character a fundamental part of the firm's hiring, retention, and promotion criteria for all professionals, regardless of service line within the firm— even at the expense of a more profitable bottom line in the short-term.*[58]

---

[58] Ibid.

Sometimes focusing on unchecked revenue growth or short-term profitability leads to dysfunctions that are merely annoying. For example, I will never be convinced that the move to open office plans was about anything other than cost savings. Sure, in a Silicon Valley start-up, it might make sense to have a bunch of young, creative people all sharing ideas in one space. On the other hand, in a public accounting firm where hundreds of professionals need to have simultaneous confidential conversations, the lack of offices with a door reduces productivity and unwittingly encourages the most senior people to work from home, where they can't mentor the more junior people.

In the worst case, losing your vision can literally make things fall apart. Allegedly Boeing began in the early 2000s to focus more on profitability than on the engineering excellence for which it was famous. More work was outsourced, and less quality control was performed. A relentless focus on the bottom line produced outsized returns for shareholders in the mid 2010s – which were lost when safety began to suffer in a product for which safety was paramount.[59] As Holman Jenkins put it:

> *In manufacturing, you get the behavior you reward. Boeing needs to get back to rewarding manufacturing teams that are quick and flawless, rather than merely quick.*[60]

Getting the behavior you reward goes beyond manufacturing. Culture could be lost in public accounting firms as well. Andersen had historically been a firm where, "What always struck me about AA was that integrity and honesty were the most important things."[61] Somewhere along the line that sense of mission got lost; by the 1990s, "We were supposedly still the guardians of the public trust, but no one ever mentioned that. Everyone did, however, talk about making money all the time."[62]

What was arguably the most mission-driven of the public accounting firms had lost its way. And the way is easily lost. Richard Kyte points out that:

---

[59] Tully, Shawn, "How Boeing Broke Down," *Fortune,* February 22, 2024. As of this writing, Boeing had been ordered to pay $2.7 billion and its CEO and chairman had stepped down over multiple safety incidents between 2018 and 2024.
[60] Jenkins, Holman, "The Boeing Just-So Story," *The Wall Street Journal*, April 23, 2024.
[61] Toffler, *Final Accounting*, "The Making of an Android."
[62] Ibid, "The Cult in Culture."

Because every organization is made up of individuals who usually enter at different times in the organization's history and bring to the place their own interests, concerns, desires, and perceptions, each one needs to discover how he or she fits into the culture. The deep story allows them to do this in a deliberate and meaningful way. If the deep story is not told on a regular basis, and if each member is not allowed the opportunity to find his or her own place within the story, even the most successfully integrated organizations that have succeeded in progressing from a collection of "I's" into a unified "we" will gradually disintegrate and fragment into a collection of "I's" once again.[63]

So it's important to first figure out what it is that really matters, and then put your money (there's that word again) where your mouth is. These days, that gets called "authenticity," which tends to remind me of the George Burns quote, "The key to success is sincerity – if you can fake that, you've got it made."[64]

In all seriousness, any organization needs to figure out what it wants its real rules to be, because those are the rules that will ultimately be followed.

I suggest there are four characteristics of real rules:

(1) People talk about them all the time;

(2) People are rewarded for following them;

(3) People are punished for not following them; and

(4) Systems and processes make them easy to follow.

One of my local parish priests likes to remind us that what you think about and what you talk about are pretty good indicators of what you care about. Lao Tzu was remarkably blunt on the subject over two thousand years ago:

---

[63] Kyte, Richard, *Ethical Business*, (Anselm Academic, 2016), "Growing Ethical Cultures."
[64] That's another one where I can't actually find a written attribution, although it's more plausible to believe Burns was speaking extemporaneously and didn't put the quote in writing than it is to believe the same of Nietzsche.

When a ruler is silent on the subject of virtue, the people are discouraged from practicing it. Meanwhile, a ruler who revels in riches encourages thievery.[65]

A colleague pointed out to me that successful chemical companies talk a lot about safety – because it matters to them. Jason Brennan cites the concrete example of Alcoa under Paul O'Neill:

Paul O'Neill ensured that safety played a role in promotion, hiring, firing, onboarding, and other decisions within ALCOA. Being a leader in safety at ALCOA was one way to move up the ranks. Being a laggard in safety was a good way to be shown the door.[66]

If your organization regularly talks about safety, rewards behavior that improves safety, and punishes behavior that reduces safety, there's a pretty good chance it cares about safety. If the organization exclusively talks about revenue and profits, that's probably what it cares about – and it may have lost sight of the values that enable it to earn revenue and profits. In *Start with Why*, Simon Sinek notes that organizations frequently measure dollars, which he defines as a "what," not a "why." The "why" is the mission of the organization, and is usually not measured in dollars. He further notes surprising examples of how successful an organization can be by actually measuring the "why" of purpose rather than the "what" of revenue – even in the counterintuitive case of a friendly debt collection agency that outperformed its more ruthless peers.[67]

Having a mission isn't about corporate donations to charity, or giving everyone a day off to provide public service, or having a vague slogan that says your mission is to do good in the world. As Brennan points out:

---

[65] Lao Tzu, *Tao Te Ching*, trans. Sam Torode and Dwight Goddard (Sam Torode Book Arts, 2021), original text 4th century BC, "Restraint."

[66] Brennan, Jason, William English, John Hasnas, and Peter Jaworski, *Business Ethics for Better Behavior* (Oxford University Press, 2021), "Psychological Factors."

[67] Sinek, Simon, *Start with Why: How Great Leaders Inspire* (Penguin Group, 2009), "Split Happens."

The most important social responsibility of business is to ensure the world is genuinely better off with that business performing its core function than without it.... You can have exceptional primary business ethics without exercising CSR [corporate social responsibility], and you can have impressive CSR despite being unethical.[68]

On the other hand, you actually have to believe your vision story. If you pretend to believe in something you don't, people will probably figure it out pretty quickly. In the multidimensional chess game of human interactions, it's probably reasonable to assume other people are selfish, jealous, shortsighted, stubborn, and ungrateful. But it's probably a bad idea to assume they're stupid and can't see through you – whether those people are your customers, your employees, or your regulators.

That's not to imply that even a mission statement that is well articulated and truly believed makes things easy. One of the world's most beloved brands, the Walt Disney Company, states that its mission is "to entertain, inform and inspire people around the globe through the power of unparalleled storytelling." I would probably have added something about "family." Or perhaps that word was deliberately omitted because as the definition of "family" has become more fluid in modern society, it's put Disney in a famously tough spot. That was probably not a spot they could avoid. Newer definitions of what a "family" looks like alienate some people. To reject those definitions alienates others. That was a decision that Disney was forced to confront.[69] I don't envy the decision makers. But knowing your core mission helps you understand what questions you truly need to answer.

---

[68] Brennan, English, Hasnas, and Jaworski, *Business Ethics for Better Behavior*, "The Business of Business is Business."
[69] Detailed from one side of the debate in Wilson Chapman's "Disney's Queer Track Record: A Troubled History," *IndieWire*, June 14, 2023.

One of the best parables around losing sight of the mission may be in Dr. Seuss' book for young environmentalists, *The Lorax*. While the anti-pollution themes are obvious, I find the most intriguing part of the story to be the antagonist, the Once-ler. The Once-ler is not a one-dimensional villain. He is a masterful entrepreneur and engineer who single-handedly builds his own factory and machines, employs his family, and produces a product (however weird it may be) that his customers want to buy. He is also not insensitive to the environmental impact of his work. As the forest creatures are driven from their homes by his industry, he reflects:

> *I, the Once-ler, felt sad as I watched them all go.*
>
> *But... business is business! And business must grow....*
>
> *I meant no harm. I most truly did not.*
>
> *But I had to grow bigger. So bigger I got.*

In the end, with the forest all cut down and no more resources to exploit, the Once-ler's family abandons him in the very vehicles he built. He is left alone with the impact of his own egotism:

> *Now all that was left 'neath the bad-smelling sky*
>
> *Was my big empty factory... the Lorax... and I....*
>
> *That was long, long ago. But each day since that day*
>
> *I've sat here and worried and worried away.*
>
> *Through the years while my buildings have fallen apart,*
>
> *I've worried about it with all of my heart.*[70]

The Once-ler focused so much on short-term revenue growth that he lost track of the mission, which at a minimum should have included something about the sustainability of the natural resources he needed to produce his product. Clearly no one else at his company cared about the mission either, since they all just stole his cars and cleared out as soon as the factory shut down. He was rewarding nothing but increased production – and he got what he rewarded.

---

[70] Geisel, Theodore Seuss, *The Lorax*, (Random House, 1971).

If you care about sustainability, you need to reward sustainability. Not as an afterthought by giving people a little sustainability badge or getting rid of the disposable paper cups in the break room, but by compensating people based on a robustly measured sustainability metric. Otherwise it's just greenwashing. I was a bit disturbed at a recent AICPA[71] conference to hear that while over 90% of public companies report sustainability metrics, almost none of them think those figures are auditable.

The same goes for quality, customer satisfaction, employee engagement, or any other measure that is core to the mission. You have to talk about it, reward it, and enable it. Arturo Bejar, former senior engineering and product leader at Facebook, says it very well:

> *Social media companies, and Meta in particular, manage their businesses based on a close and ongoing analysis of data. Nothing gets changed unless it is measured. Once Meta establishes metrics for anything, employees are given concrete incentives to drive those metrics in the direction the company deems useful and valuable. Metrics determine, for example, how many people work in a given department. Most of all, metrics establish the companies' priorities.[72]*

---

[71] American Institute of Certified Public Accountants. Also the Association of International Certified Professional Accountants, "the global voice of the accounting and finance profession, founded by the American Institute of CPAs" (per aicpa-cima.com). No, it's not confusing at all that the same organization uses the same acronym for two different things.

[72] Bejar, Arturo and Jonathan Haidt, "How to Reduce the Sexual Solicitation of Teens on Instagram," *After Babel*, May 6, 2024, **https://www.afterbabel.com/p/make-social-media-safe-for-teens**.

That's not just true for social media companies – that's true for everyone. Legend has it that in the Soviet Union, a nail factory was ordered to maximize the total number of nails it produced. The manager quickly realized that he could most effectively do that by producing lots of tiny nails, which were mostly useless. The incentive was then changed to maximize the total *weight* of the nails. The manager responded by producing nothing but railroad spikes, which were also mostly useless. The story may or may not be true,[73] but it gets the point across that you get what you measure.[74]

Enabling the mission means more than saying that it's important, and even more than putting incentives in place. It also means establishing systems and processes that make it not just possible, but easy, to do the right thing. For example, I tell my catechism students constantly about the importance of the sacrament of confession. Unfortunately, most parishes don't make the sacrament available very often. That's a problem because people (including me) don't like going to confession. It's embarrassing. And if there's an excuse for not going, like it being offered only once a week at an inconvenient time, that makes it even less likely that people will go. By contrast, I've visited a few churches from Dublin to rural Virginia that offered confession daily before Mass. It took away the excuses.

---

[73] It seems to have first occurred in a 1957 Newsweek article.
[74] Brennan makes a convincing case that this is true even in the "ivory tower" of academia. He posits that the massive cost increases and growing dysfunction of academia are due not to "corporatism" or "woke ideology," but simply to academics and administrators having bad incentives. Brennan, Jason and Phillip Magness, *Cracks in the Ivory Tower* (Oxford University Press, 2019).

People may be selfish, but they aren't stupid. If you say something is important but make it hard to comply with, they'll figure out that it isn't really all that important. The same is true if you stick it in a mission statement or values statement somewhere but leadership never talks about it, never rewards people for doing it, and never punishes people for not doing it (or only punishes the most serious lapses). We all respond to the incentives we're given. The director of revenue accounting at my big audit client in the pre-Enron days called me "the most auditor-like auditor" she'd ever met. (I said, "Thank you." She said she didn't mean it as a compliment. I said, "I know.") Even so, I found my approach to analyzing financial statements changed when I switched to providing due diligence for investors, because my goal had changed to identifying potential problems with the investment thesis, rather than signing off on the financial statements. Even if you're the most "auditor-like-auditor," it's easier to take a hard line when the people you're examining aren't the ones paying you to come back next year.[75]

A successful mission-driven campaign engages the emotions, as well as incentives. Mothers Against Drunk Driving did a masterful job in the 1980s of changing the conversation around drinking and driving. The organization combined a push for tougher laws and penalties with an appeal to conscience, successfully creating social stigma around driving under the influence. In my compliance role I frequently contrasted DUI, which is generally perceived as immoral, with speeding, which is generally not. Most people avoid driving under the influence not just because they might get a ticket, but because they believe it's wrong. Further, the popularization of "designated driver" programs engaged the fourth characteristic of a "real rule" by making it easier to comply.

---

[75] As it turns out, sometimes it's okay to be tough on the target of due diligence. It was an article of faith in my office that I could never serve a particular company as a client because I'd made so many mean observations when I was analyzing them. One partner disagreed and took me to meet the CFO when the company was contemplating a major transaction. The CFO and I looked at each other, and he said, "Does this mean you'll do all the stuff to our counterparty that you did to me?" I smiled and nodded and he smiled back and said, "Welcome aboard." I went on to do millions of dollars of work for him on multiple transactions. In my experience, "tough but fair" usually works out in the end in my profession.

In the end, we all have selfish tendencies. We're wired that way and we need to accept that fact. But our selfishness can be managed and directed. One way to do so in an organization is with a sense of mission – of something larger than oneself, that can serve as a moral anchor. That mission can direct the human will outside of the self to something bigger. We must, of course, be careful in choosing the moral anchor, which can lead to concluding that the ends justify the means (which we will explore in more detail in Chapter Four). The physician Carl Elliott notes that doctors may sometimes do awful things if they believe them to be justified:

> *The forces of social conformity are especially powerful in organizations that are driven by a deep sense of moral purpose. If the aims of the organization are righteous, its members feel, it is wrong to put barriers in the way.*[76]

Indeed, many years ago I researched the idea that Nazism had quasi-religious characteristics that made it a moral anchor for its adherents. It was just a really, really bad one. Not every mission about which people feel passionately is equally laudable.

Even when the mission is good, the selfish nature of humanity comes through easily. My wife and I have worked for various church groups for many years, and the people who work there can still be selfish despite the intrinsically moral mission of the organization. That can turn people off from the church and other non-profits, as we learn that self-seeking and backstabbing still occur there. It's important to remember that any organization, no matter how noble its goals, is still composed of flawed humans. The fact that profitability isn't the goal of the enterprise doesn't mean that human nature is somehow changed.

---

[76] Elliott, Carl, "In Medicine, the Morally Unthinkable Too Easily Comes to Seem Normal," *The New York Times*, May 7, 2024. Dr. Elliott cites the research of Irving Janis on the dangers of groupthink.

Still, most organizations compound the problem, losing sight of that underlying mission through the easy metric of monetization. The real tragedy is that not only doesn't money buy happiness, but neither does our selfishness. Past a certain (fairly low) point, material wealth doesn't correlate well with emotional well-being. Adam and Eve were kicked out of paradise for their selfishness – a metaphor for humanity if ever there was one.

II. Jealous

> "Human souls long for praise, and people
> pay great attention to this world and the
> positions and wealth it offers. As a rule,
> they feel no desire for virtue and have no
> special interest in virtuous people."
>
> - Ibn Khaldun[77]

"Human souls long for praise." So much so that if they feel slighted, they might kill someone over it – even their own family. The second story of Genesis takes us from the first sin, pride, to the second, jealousy. The example of Cain and Abel is so striking not just because Cain murders his brother, but because of how profoundly stupid and counterproductive it is.

Again, to me this story is clearly allegorical. After the murder, Cain is afraid that "whoever finds me will kill me."[78] If we're biblical literalists, there are only three people on Earth at this point, Cain and his parents. So once again, this is not history, but a lesson about human nature. Cain was angry because God preferred Abel's sacrifice to his. Did he think God was going to like him better after he killed his brother? It certainly didn't work out that way.

It's tempting to think that Cain was uniquely awful in his jealousy, and certainly killing your brother is pretty bad. But jealousy is hardly confined to him, or other horrible people. Everyone, even quite good people, suffer from it. In fact, while Jesus was telling his disciples that he would have to suffer and die for mankind's salvation, they were busy arguing with each other over who among them was the greatest.[79]

---

[77] Ibn Khaldun, *The Muqaddimah,* trans. Franz Rosenthal (Princeton University Press, 1967), original text 1377, Book One.
[78] Genesis 4:14.
[79] Mark 9:31-34.

The lesson here is that humans are extremely status conscious. That makes sense, because humans are social animals, and status is important to social animals. As with other primates like gorillas and chimpanzees, status directly affects things that are critically important for evolution, like your selection of mates or indeed whether you get to reproduce at all.[80] What's interesting, though, is that our genetic "hardwiring" seems to mean that the status drive continues even when it no longer serves any useful purpose.

For example, not too long ago I was going to be moved from a domestic leadership role in the partnership to a global deputy role. It was more of a "side-motion" than either a promotion or demotion. But the most interesting thing was my reaction to losing the domestic role. With that role, I was one of the select group of partners who directly set compensation for other partners. And I found that I didn't want to give up that power.

That was a fascinating thing about me for a couple of reasons. First, I didn't actually like setting compensation for other partners. The process was always rushed, I was obsessively concerned with fairness to the point of losing sleep over it, and I really didn't enjoy communicating the outcomes to my team because someone inevitably felt slighted. Second, there was no practical benefit to me from the status that came with the role. I was making more than enough money to get my kids through college, live a comfortable lifestyle, and donate to the charities I wanted to support. The role change wouldn't have reduced my compensation. And I didn't need the status for biological reasons – I have four children and trust me, I'm not looking to reproduce anymore.

So why did I have a viscerally negative reaction to losing authority that I didn't enjoy having? Because as a social primate, I'm biologically wired to protect my status, even if it doesn't make any sense to do so. Oddly enough, I've been complimented by team members for my humility and approachability – which isn't very consistent with my evident status-seeking behavior. The only way I can reconcile those data points is by concluding that almost everyone is status-seeking, and I may actually be a little less so than most.

~~~

---

[80] Wright, *The Moral Animal*, "Social Status."

Let's tweak that last thought a bit.

Perhaps an even better conclusion is that "almost everyone of high status is status-seeking." It stands to reason that most people who achieve high status probably do so at least in part because they care about it. A logical corollary would be that the higher someone's status, the likelier it is to be important to them. And since it's a well-established point of psychology that people generally have a stronger drive to avoid loss than to achieve gain,[81] once someone has status, they're going to cling to it like a cat with its claws sunk into the rug. Even if it doesn't really make a lot of sense, as in my case.

Status takes different forms. It might be money, or power, or fame, or the acclaim of peers. Returning to the allegations against Ariely and Gino, and broader issues of academic dishonesty, a recent article asked the question:

> *To what extent is dishonesty a matter of character, and to what extent a matter of situation? Research misconduct is sometimes explained away by incentives—the publishing requirements for the job market, or the acclaim that can lead to consulting fees and Davos appearances. As one senior faculty member told me, of bridging the academic and corporate worlds, "You see what the money can buy you, you fly business class on work trips. It tickles you in that little place, and you need to have more of it."[82]*

We humans are driven to seek status, and also driven to award it. There need to be leaders. Ibn Khaldun observes:

> *Ranks are widely distributed among people, and there are various levels of rank among them. This is God's wise plan with regard to His creation... The existence and persistence of the human species can materialize only through the cooperation of all men in behalf of what is good for them... Therefore, it is imperative to make them cooperate...[83]*

---

[81] See for example Kahneman, Daniel and Amos Tversky, "Loss Aversion in Riskless Choice: A Reference-Dependent Model," *The Quarterly Journal of Economics Vol.106, No. 4*, November 1991.

[82] Lewis-Kraus, Gideon, "They Studied Dishonesty. Was Their Work a Lie?" *The New Yorker*, September 30, 2023.

[83] Ibn Khaldun, *The Muqaddimah,* Ch.5.

If you've ever seen a group try to accomplish anything by committee, you know it tends not to go well. That holds true whether it's a group of kids trying to organize a game on the playground, an army in battle, or a business. Someone has to be in charge. Thus the insistence by the ancient Israelites on having a king in the first book of Samuel. Of course that king, Saul, decided that he didn't need to listen to anyone – even God – and had his decapitated corpse nailed to a wall for his arrogance.[84]

Modern coups against business leaders don't generally end with anyone being beheaded. CEOs tend more to be reviled in the press for excessive compensation, which may be annoying to them but is a lot less fatal. Of course, CEO compensation is an interesting question that is perhaps relevant to our analysis of jealousy. A study by the Economic Policy Institute shows that CEOs of U.S. public companies earned 344 times as much as the average worker in 2022, up from a 21:1 ratio in 1965.[85] The Economic Policy Institute attributes that increase to capture of public company boards by management, but I'm not sure that's necessarily true. It could also be rationally explained by the growing size and complexity of public companies.

---

[84] 1 Samuel 31:8-10.

[85] Bivens, Josh and Jori Kandra, "CEO pay declined slightly in 2022," *Economic Policy Institute*, September 21, 2023. The time-series graph in the paper shows an exponentially increasing curve from 1965 – 2000, peaking at 381, with a relatively flat ratio (with considerable ups and downs in particular years) in the following 22 years.

According to Wikipedia, the 50 largest companies in the world have median revenue of $236 billion, with a median profit margin[86] of 5.25%, or $12.4 billion.[87] Let's hypothesize that the difference between the best CEO and the next best CEO is an incremental profit margin of just 0.1%, raising the margin from 5.25% to 5.35%. For the median company in the top 50, that's an increased profit of $236 million just from a 0.1% increase in profitability. And it's not unreasonable to expect that the best CEO could produce at least that much of a difference in profitability, is it? Indeed, when Starbucks announced that it had poached Chipotle's successful CEO, its stock price shot up 24.5% while Chipotle's fell 7.5%.[88] A study by Quigley and Hambrick suggests that the right CEO is seen as an increasingly important contributor to corporate performance.[89]

In some ways that makes perfect sense. After all, the very best basketball players or football players can make a huge difference in team performance. I don't think anyone would claim the Chicago Bulls or New England Patriots would have dominated their leagues without Michael Jordan or Tom Brady, respectively. To some extent, that reliance on a key individual may well extend to other domains. Iconic leaders in politics and business such as George Washington or Steve Jobs almost certainly achieved outcomes no one else would have.

Most of us don't mind seeing Michael Jordan or Tom Brady being greatly rewarded for their exceptional skill. So why doesn't it make sense that a CEO might take home half of that 0.1% incremental value – which would amount to $118 million per year in our calculation above, far more than the actual average CEO pay?

---

[86] "Profit margin" in this case refers to net income divided by revenue, not gross margin which is gross profit divided by revenue.

[87] "List of largest companies by revenue," Wikimedia Foundation, last modified January 27, 2025, https://en.wikipedia.org/wiki/List_of_largest_companies_by_revenue, citing Fortune 500 Global 2023 ranking. I took the median profitability percentage and multiplied it by the median revenue to arrive at median net income, which gives a slightly different number than taking the median net income. The theory remains the same however you calculate it, and the numbers aren't meaningfully different.

[88] Cohen, Ben, "There's a new $27 Billion CEO – and He Might Actually Be Worth It," *The Wall Street Journal*, August 24, 2024.

[89] Quigley, Timothy J. and Donald C. Hambrick, "Has the 'CEO effect' increased in recent decades?" *Strategic Management Journal*, March 12, 2014.

I suggest there are three flaws in this "winner take all" approach to executive compensation:

1. Success in a large company is attributable to a huge number of people.

2. There's little guarantee that the CEO is in fact the best leader available.

3. Excessive concentration of power creates dynamics of jealousy that are inherently harmful to the organization.

Let's take them in order.

Each basketball team puts five people on the court at one time. A football team has eleven on the field. It's pretty easy to assess the performance of one individual. If a basketball player scores thirty points per game (Michael Jordan's average) compared to around ten points per game for an average NBA player, that makes a huge difference of twenty points, which is decisive given a typical point spread of around ten points per game.

On the other hand, the median number of employees at the top 50 companies cited above was 220,000. Granted, we would expect the CEO to have a much higher impact on profitability than the average employee. But mathematically, the average employee impact on performance works out to 0.0005%. For the CEO to move profitability by the seemingly trivial 0.1% I postulated above, they would have to have two hundred times the impact of the average employee.

And maybe they do. Except...

There are a few pretty good reasons to suspect leaders are frequently not in fact the single most qualified individual for the job. The most obvious is the famous "Peter Principle," set out by Laurence Peter and Raymond Hull.[90] At its simplest, it asserts that people are promoted to their level of incompetence. Peter asserts that inevitably, as surely as the sun rises in the east, individuals who are competent will be promoted, until they eventually come to rest at their level of incompetence, where they can't be promoted further. While the principle is most famously elucidated by Peter and Hull, they in no way invented the concept. Nearly a hundred years earlier, Gilbert and Sullivan's comic opera "H.M.S. Pinafore" described the ascent of the First Lord of the British Admiralty, probably the single most important military officer in the world at the time. The fictional First Lord began his career as an office boy and proceeded through a steady stream of promotions, none of which involved naval service. At the end of his autobiographical song, he declares:

> *Now landsmen all, whoever you may be,*
>
> *If you want to rise to the top of the tree,*
>
> *If your soul isn't fettered to an office stool,*
>
> *Be careful to be guided by this golden rule:*
>
> *Stick close to your desk and never go to sea,*
>
> *And you all may be rulers of the Queen's Navy![91]*

The song parodied the actual First Lord of the Admiralty at the time, William Henry Smith, who had never gone to sea in his life.

Sometimes the application of the Peter Principle is dramatic. I had a junior employee who was promoted to the next level based on her stunning competence. She then proved to be equally strikingly incompetent at the next level – unable and unwilling to do anything beyond her previous role. Usually the effect isn't so extreme. Someone who was good at their previous job is simply mediocre at the next one.

---

[90] Peter, Laurence and Raymond Hull, *The Peter Principle* (Harper Business, 2009), original text 1969.

[91] Gilbert, W.S. and Arthur Sullivan, *H.M.S. Pinafore*, 1878, "When I Was a Lad."

Human resources organizations devote a fair amount of time and attention to battling the Peter Principle. For example, the "nine box" talent grid attempts to evaluate an individual's suitability both for their current job and separately for promotion. The nine box model categorizes people into groups such as "solid performers" who should be retained but not promoted further, "diamonds in the rough" who should be developed for higher ranks, and "superstars" who are effective at both their current and future levels. That certainly sounds right, and I participated in a fair number of nine box assessments. Of course, if you Google "nine box talent grid," the first hit (at least when I did it) is, "**9 Box grid is sh*t. Here's why ...**"[92] The author of the post, Haricharan Vijayaraghavan, cynically suggests that the nine box simply measures doing a good job on one axis, and whether your manager likes you on the other. Vijayaraghavan notes that "If predicting potential was so easy, we will not see so many leaders fail so consistently."

And that suggests another concern with the right people getting into the right roles. It seems highly plausible that in a large organization, successfully climbing the greasy pole may reflect more skill at greasy-pole-climbing than at actually leading the organization. Ibn Khaldun observes:

> *Consequently, a person who seeks and desires rank must be obsequious and use flattery as powerful men and rulers require. Otherwise, it will be impossible for him to obtain any rank.*[93]

The larger an organization gets, the more political it becomes. And as Tocqueville observes, politicians tend not to be paragons of virtue or talent: "When I stepped ashore in the United States, I discovered with amazement to what extent merit was common among the governed but rare among the rulers."[94]

As Laurence Peter adds, with tongue only slightly in cheek,

---

[92] **https://www.linkedin.com/pulse/9-box-grid-sht-heres-why-haricharan-vijayaraghavan/**
[93] Ibn Khaldun, *The Muqaddimah*, Ch.5. It's fascinating how much of modern socioeconomics Ibn Khaldun anticipated. In this example, he precedes Laurence Peter's observations by six hundred years. He also anticipated Marx's labor theory of value by five centuries (compare Chapter 5 of the Muqaddimah to Chapter 2 of Karl Marx's *Das Kapital*, Volume 1, 1867).
[94] De Tocqueville, Alexis, *Democracy in America Vol.1*, trans. Gerald E. Bevan (Penguin Books, 2003), original text 1835, "Government by Democracy in America."

So we see that exceptional leadership competence cannot make its way within an established hierarchy.... an employee's competence is assessed, not by disinterested observers like you and me, but by the employer or – more likely nowadays – by other employees on higher ranks of the same hierarchy. In their eyes, leadership potential is insubordination, and insubordination is incompetence.[95]

Bad leadership is not a new phenomenon. The Roman Empire famously had a succession of lousy emperors, starting with Nero, whose death was followed by four emperors in a single year. After an 84-year run of good leaders, the empire then experienced another disaster with Commodus, followed by a year with five emperors (four in one year apparently not having been enough). The Severan dynasty that resulted was marked by Edward Gibbon as the beginning of the decline and fall of the Roman Empire.[96] It's noteworthy that not only were most of the leaders wicked and incompetent, but they tended to be short-lived, frequently assassinated by their successors or the very Praetorian Guard assigned to protect them. And yet, jealousy and ambition drove a succession of unwise men to claw their way into power and make unwise decisions that proved ruinous to their nation.

---

[95] Peter and Hull, *The Peter Principle*, "Followers and Leaders."
[96] Gibbon, Edward, *History of the Decline and Fall of the Roman Empire* (Kindle edition by B&R Samizdat Express), original text 1776.

As Vijayaraghavan observed, the number of modern leaders who make spectacularly bad decisions is too long to list. Indeed, the same Wall Street Journal article that highlighted the market's exuberant reaction to Starbucks' new CEO pointed out that the market is often proven wrong in those assessments.[97] Now, perhaps that's unfair. Unlike sports stars, who play in a tightly constrained environment with few variables, a business leader or politician is operating in an environment of almost infinite complexity. Geopolitical changes, technological changes, regulatory changes, a swing in exchange rates, a natural disaster, or any number of other unpredictable factors might undermine even the most brilliant executive. But the converse is also true. An executive might seem brilliant due to nothing more than luck. And they can always deflect blame due to factors outside their control. People rarely show much self-awareness with respect to their competence.[98] Most famous athletes keep playing well past their prime, when they should logically be retiring to enjoy their hard-earned fortunes. Isn't it then reasonable to suspect, as Laurence Peter suggested, that many executives are working above their level of competence, frequently without knowing it? Even worse may be if they do know it – research suggests that "power paired with incompetence leads to aggression" because "aggression by power holders who perceive themselves as incompetent is driven by ego defensiveness."[99]

Perhaps that's all just a little too cynical for you. So let's stipulate that a good executive can add considerable value to an organization, and that most of the people in leadership roles are better qualified for that role than the average person.[100]

---

[97] Cohen, "There's a New $27 Billion CEO – and He Might Actually Be Worth It."

[98] Again with tongue only partially in cheek, The Peter Principle suggests in its chapter on "Health & Happiness at Zero PQ" that people are happiest when they're unaware of their incompetence.

[99] Fast, Nathanael and Serena Chen, "When the Boss Feels Inadequate," *Psychological Science, 20(11)*, 2009.

[100] Recent research suggests the first part of that statement is likely true but the second part may not be. While good managers have a significantly positive impact on team productivity, people who push to be in leadership roles tend to be worse at it than randomly selected individuals. Weidman, Ben, Joseph Vecci, Farah Said, David J. Deming, and Sonia R. Bhalotra, "How Do You Find a Good Manager," *National Bureau of Economic Research*, July 2024.

The operation of human jealousy still means that their desire for power will be problematic. As Lord Acton famously said in his 1887 letter to Bishop Creighton, "Power tends to corrupt and absolute power corrupts absolutely." Even good people will do bad things to retain their position, potentially acting against the interests of their constituents.

I found a fairly typical example in my career in mergers and acquisitions. I led one of the first sell-side due diligence projects in the United States about twenty years ago.[101] Sell-side due diligence is a rigorous analysis of the business undertaken for the seller, but from a potential buyer's perspective. It helps identify any warts in advance. At the end of the exercise, my client's CEO told me he'd learned more about his company from my analysis than he had in years of running the business. Armed with that knowledge, I tried to introduce a concept of "risk diligence" into the marketplace – performing sell-side due diligence to evaluate the company's weaknesses for management or the board of directors when no transaction was imminent. I failed miserably. Later attempts by other partners to rebrand the initiative as "activist shareholder defense" were no more successful.

Why?

Because one of two things would inevitably happen:

1. The diligence exercise discovers nothing of interest, in which case the sponsor of the exercise at the company has wasted money; or, worse,

2. The diligence exercise does uncover issues. The problem then becomes that the sponsor, who would usually be the Chief Financial Officer, didn't find those issues themselves but instead the problems were found by an outside advisor. Rather than look like an idiot, the potential sponsor prefers not to know what the issues might be.

---

[101] Vendor due diligence, the European equivalent, has existed longer, although it's hard to find an exact date for when it entered common use.

Ironically enough, that episode didn't just prove the jealousy of CFOs. It also proved mine. After I had tried to sell the work a few times and failed, I gave up and went back to focusing on my day job. I described the situation to a colleague whose judgment I trusted. She suggested that perhaps someone else would be successful at developing the practice, and asked if I would be happy about that. I told her I wouldn't be. It was my idea, and I didn't want someone else taking it forward without me and getting the credit. She was surprised and disappointed in me. I think the example illustrates how jealousy corrupts even the aspirational sense of mission from the prior chapter. I thought the service would add quality and transparency to the financial system. I thought it would be a powerful extension of the objective analysis that lies at the heart of public accounting. But I also wanted it to be mine.

We're all jealous, not just CEOs or CFOs. We all want credit for our ideas. We all want to hold on to any status, perk, or privilege we've earned. Or that we think we've earned. Whether it's an assigned parking space, or an office with a door, or an "employee of the month" plaque, or credit for an idea – we will jealously protect and fight for whatever we think belongs to us. And it makes good evolutionary sense, because status confers authority, and people obey those in authority. Robert Cialdini's book *Influence* describes not just the infamous Milgram experiment where an authority figure successfully induced the vast majority of subjects to administer what they thought were terrifyingly painful electrical shocks, but also numerous other situations where titles, clothing, or other status markers persuaded people to comply with unreasonable requests.[102]

And it's reasonable to assume that the stakes get higher at higher status levels. The more unequal the distribution of power, the bigger the prizes, the harder people will fight. They may pretend, or even believe, that they're acting for the good of the organization, but they're probably really looking out for themselves. Robert Wright explains it bluntly:

---

[102] Cialdini, Robert B., *Influence* (Collins Business, 2007), "Authority."

*And there is little evidence that high-status people have any
particular proclivity toward conscience or sacrifice. Indeed,
the new paradigm stresses that they have attained their
status not for "the good of the group" but for themselves;
they can be expected to use it accordingly, just as they can
be expected to pretend otherwise.*[103]

Returning to Lord Acton, the more power is vested in leadership, the worse
the situation is likely to become. Tocqueville, a French aristocrat who lived
through Napoleon's regime and whose parents narrowly escaped the
guillotine during the Reign of Terror, had fairly strong views on the
concentration of power:

*Omnipotence seems self-evidently a bad and dangerous
thing. Its exercise appears to be beyond man's powers,
whoever he might be, and I see that only God can be
omnipotent without danger because his wisdom and justice
are always equal to his power. There is, therefore, no
earthly authority so worthy of respect or vested with so
sacred a right that I wish to allow it unlimited action and
unrestricted dominance."*[104]

~~~

You don't need to have all-encompassing power or riches to be jealous of
your privileges. An IRS agent, highway patrol officer, local prosecutor, or
clerk at the Department of Motor Vehicles may not be rich or powerful in the
conventional sense, but within the scope of their control, their authority may
be almost total. And those individuals may well be just as jealous as a
dictator or CEO.

---

[103] Wright, *The Moral Animal*, "Evolutionary Ethics."
[104] De Tocqueville, *Democracy in America*, "The Majority in the United States Is All-
Powerful and the Consequences of That."

The reason I focus on jealousy at leadership levels is not because it's more prevalent there (although I suspect it may be), but because the effects of this vice that affects us all are more dangerous there simply because those individuals' scope of control is broader. And I'll return consistently to Tocqueville and the U.S. Founding Fathers on the topic of power and jealousy because they understood it so well. Perhaps witnessing the American and French revolutions gave them a unique perspective on how people clawed their way to the top, and how rare humility really is in a leader.

"A tremendously self-aware man, Washington knew that he was a deeply flawed person himself... This made him humble in his duties."[105] Certainly I didn't fully appreciate the unique excellence of George Washington's refusal to stand for a third presidential term until I'd lived in Mexico and Chile.

The first president of independent Mexico, Agustín de Iturbide, declared himself emperor, began to live extravagantly, and was ultimately executed. Guadalupe Victoria was the only president in the first thirty years of Mexico's independence to actually complete his term – the rest were ejected in power struggles, some lasting as little as six days in office. The next president to serve a full term was the celebrated Benito Juarez, who served 14 years (!)

Early Chilean leaders lasted longer, but their story is no less colored with jealousy. Chile's George Washington equivalent was the revolutionary hero and Supreme Director Bernardo O'Higgins. He had his fellow revolutionary heroes José Miguel Carrera and Manuel Rodriguez executed. O'Higgins was deposed in a coup led by Ramón Freire, formerly his closest ally.[106]

Business isn't the same as national politics, but in large enough entities it can start to look pretty similar. Tocqueville, who was something between a conservative and a classical liberal, and certainly no Marxist, observed that labor relations could easily harden into an aristocracy, and a pretty ruthless one at that:

---

[105] Valsania, Maurizio, "How George Washington Used His First Thanksgiving as President to Unite a New Country," *Oregon Capital Chronicle*, November 28, 2024.
[106] Sepúlveda, Alfredo, "Bernardo O'Higgins: The Rebel Son of a Victory," *Society for Irish Latin American Studies*, 2006, **https://www.irlandeses.org/0610_206to215.pdf**.

> *The industrialist only asks the worker for his labor and the*
> *latter only expects his wages. The one is not committed to*
> *protect, nor the other to defend; they are not linked in any*
> *permanent way, either by habit or duty. This business*
> *aristocracy seldom lives among the industrial population it*
> *manages; it aims not to rule them but to use them.*[107]

How then to address the concentration of power and the jealousy it inspires? Tocqueville and the Founding Fathers had some pretty good ideas. It's probably no coincidence that the United States constitution has lasted 235 years as of this writing.

To begin, James Madison suggested limiting the scope of control, which safeguards against the corruption of power and jealousy:

> *They will see, therefore, that in all cases where power is to*
> *be conferred, the point first to be decided is, whether such a*
> *power be necessary to the public good; as the next will be, in*
> *case of an affirmative decision, to guard as effectually as*
> *possible against a perversion of the power to the public*
> *detriment.*[108]

Someone has to exercise control in any complex endeavor, or nothing gets done. Pope Leo XIII, who set the pattern for modern Catholic social teaching, acknowledged that not only was inequality a fact, but it was a necessary fact. Those with the skills to lead should lead, and that will inevitably create a degree of inequality:

---

[107] De Tocqueville, *Democracy in America*, "How an Aristocracy May Emerge from Industry."
[108] Madison, James, *The Federalist Papers*, Federalist 41, 1788.

There naturally exist among mankind manifold differences of the most important kind; people differ in capacity, skill, health, strength; and unequal fortune is a necessary result of unequal condition. Such unequality is far from being disadvantageous either to individuals or to the community. Social and public life can only be maintained by means of various kinds of capacity for business and the playing of many parts.[109]

Someone has to be in charge, whether organizing a company or a pick-up basketball game. People with the desire and capacity for control will naturally try to move to the top of the hierarchy. That is unavoidable and probably even desirable. But the scope of control should be kept as limited as possible, with appropriate checks and balances, such as the separation of powers of the U.S. government.

Because people are jealous, they will seek power. They will try to retain the power they've amassed. And they will abuse the power they have in order to hold on to it, ultimately being controlled by their very jealousy. Cain was controlled by his jealousy, and it destroyed him. The exercise of absolute power corrupted even some of the most heroic figures in the Bible, such as King David and King Solomon. Once David had consolidated control over the united Kingdom of Israel, he slept with the wife of one of his trusted warriors, then sent the warrior to the front lines to be killed.[110] Solomon, by biblical tradition the wisest man of all time, became so rich and powerful that in his arrogance he turned away from his God, and as a result his kingdom was divided.[111]

Per Simone Weil:

Force is as pitiless to the man who possesses it, or thinks he does, as it is to its victims; the second it crushes, the first it intoxicates. The truth is, nobody really possesses it.[112]

---

[109] Pope Leo XIII, *Rerum Novarum,* Encyclical on Capital and Labor, 1891. It's maybe not shocking that the leader of one of the most famously hierarchical organizations in the world supported hierarchy, but his point remains valid.
[110] 2 Samuel 11.
[111] 1 Kings 11.
[112] Weil, *Memorable Quotations*, originally appearing in *The Iliad or the Poem of Force,* 1941.

Governance is famously hard. It's hard enough to govern yourself – just ask King David, or King Solomon, or Saint Paul. It's really hard to govern an organization. You have to motivate people so they drive towards the mission without succumbing to laziness (more on laziness in the next chapter). But you have to avoid backstabbing (hopefully not in the literal sense of Cain and Abel). I believe one key to limiting the jealousy that naturally arises is to ensure the group experiences success together, rather than seeking to dominate each other. A strategy to minimize the risk of a "winner take all" approach could include the following elements:

(1) Limit the scope of control;

(2) Don't pit people against each other;

(3) Align the interests of the governing and the governed; and

(4) Use oversight to check absolute power.

If we start from Acton's principle that power is corrupting, and extend that to saying that the desire to obtain and retain power is corrupting, then the first step in avoiding toxic levels of jealousy should be to limit the amount of power at issue. In Cain and Abel's case, they were vying for divine favor. The stakes were pretty high. Ironically, they both lost. Abel died before having children, and the line of Cain's descendants ended after a few generations. According to the Bible, modern humanity is descended from Seth, Adam and Eve's third child, who was born to replace Abel.[113]

If we can lower the stakes, it may be possible to at least mitigate the toxicity of jealousy. As James Madison noted, beginning with the question of whether power needs to be conferred at all should be step one. If power is required, it should be as limited as possible to get the job done. Pope Leo XIII, who as noted above was no friend to anarchy or *laissez faire*, stated:

> *The limits must be determined by the nature of the occasion which calls for the law's interference - the principle being that the law must not undertake more, nor proceed further, than is required for the remedy of the evil or the removal of the mischief.*[114]

---

[113] Genesis 4:25.
[114] Pope Leo XIII, *Rerum Novarum,* Encyclical on Capital and Labor, 1891.

While Leo was referring specifically to the role of the state, the same logic applies to any form of control. That includes how much control is exercised by any individual. The principle of subsidiarity recommends that control be exercised in the most localized and limited way possible to achieve the required objective. Pope Pius XI, building forty years later on Leo's encyclical, continued:

> *Just as it is gravely wrong to take from individuals what they can accomplish by their own initiative and industry and give it to the community, so also it is an injustice and at the same time a grave evil and disturbance of right order to assign to a greater and higher association what lesser and subordinate organizations can do.*[115]

Of course, it's natural for status-seeking people and organizations to concentrate power and build empires, including biting off more than they can chew. I can't quite come up with an English phrase that manages the Spanish, "El que mucho abarca poco aprieta," but it translates to something like, "He who seeks much grasps little." Perhaps the most often cited English version is attributed (apparently falsely) to Thomas Jefferson: "That government is best which governs least."[116]

Again, I don't mean to advocate for anarchy, or unregulated commerce guided solely by the "invisible hand." Common misuse of his phrase notwithstanding, Adam Smith was quite realistic about the selfishness of market participants and did not advocate complete deregulation. For example, he noted that capitalists "seldom meet together, even for merriment or diversion, but the conversation ends in a conspiracy against the public, or in some contrivance to raise prices."[117]

---

[115] Pope Pius XI, *Quadragesimo Anno*, Encyclical on Reconstruction of the Social Order, 1931.
[116] Monticello.org indicates that while this quote has been attributed to Jefferson since 1853, there's no evidence he ever said it. **https://www.monticello.org/research-education/thomas-jefferson-encyclopedia/government-best-which-governs-least-spurious-quotation/**.
[117] Smith, Adam, *The Wealth of Nations*, 1776, Ch.X.

So not only does someone have to be in charge, but someone also has to provide oversight over obnoxious behavior. Leo XIII and Pius XI were both very clear on that point. My point is simply that the more an individual (or an organization) controls, the greater their potential scope for corruption and jealousy – so limiting the scope of control to the minimum required is an important safeguard.

The second safeguard is to avoid constructs that deliberately turn people against each other. Again, excessive competition that reaches the level of back-biting can be not only unproductive, but counterproductive. Jonathan Haidt gives an interesting example from the poultry industry. As it turns out, the individual hens that lay the most eggs also tend to be the most aggressive. If you breed the best individual egg-layers, they fight and you get a bunch of dead and injured hens, which hurts overall production. Research by William Muir showed that it was better to breed the whole cageful of hens who collectively had the highest egg production, rather than the best individual egg-layers. That resulted in much lower mortality and higher overall production.[118]

Humans aren't hens. But I wouldn't want to bet on us being any less vicious – or, to use the common term for jealous behavior, "political."

---

[118] Haidt, *The Righteous Mind*, "Why Are We So Groupish?"

One way to turn people against each other includes "winner take all" compensation structures, such as for example when a CEO makes 344 times as much as the average employee. Historically, attempts to regulate pay haven't fared well in Western democracies. In 2013 Switzerland attempted to cap CEO pay at 12 times the average worker's compensation. The referendum failed with almost two thirds of the Swiss public voting against.[119] That was probably for the best. I have little confidence that legislators or regulators know the "right" level of executive compensation, or the right way to calculate it. Unintended consequences leap readily to mind, such as gaming the system by outsourcing or offshoring lower paying jobs in order to raise the compensation of the "average" worker. However, a company voluntarily implementing a relatively flatter compensation structure would probably not only create more of a "we" mindset throughout the organization, but also help mitigate the backstabbing behavior that can arise when getting that extra few inches up the greasy pole makes all the difference in power and compensation.

To be clear, I'm a capitalist. It's an empirical fact that no system has lifted more people out of poverty than the free market.[120] And I believe in incentives, because as we established in the last chapter, people are selfish. Commissions and bonuses are good ways of incentivizing behavior. Stock based compensation is a great way of aligning incentives. A former colleague of mine is a director at Ownership Works, a non-profit that encourages "business leaders and investors to provide all employees with the opportunity to participate in the value they help create."[121] That seems like a great idea to me.

---

[119] Garofolo, Pat, "What We Can Learn From Switzerland's CEO Pay Cap Vote," *U.S. News*, November 25, 2013.
[120] See for example Zitelmann, Rainer, "Anyone Who Doesn't Know the Following Facts About Capitalism Should Learn Them," *Forbes*, July 27, 2020.
[121] https://www.linkedin.com/company/ownershipworks/.

Of course, none of this is easy. Leaning too heavily on monetary incentives can have the negative consequences discussed in the previous chapter, where money rather than mission becomes the whole purpose of the organization. Furthermore, people will find ways to game the system. There's a reason why in 2022 the SEC had to mandate "clawback" policies on incentive compensation[122] – recovering bonuses awarded if a subsequent accounting restatement changes the results the bonus was based on.

Incentives must also be carefully monitored to avoid creating a culture of backstabbing. A quick and easy way of turning people against each other is forced ranking systems, especially those that require termination of lower performers. Those systems tend to rely on monetary measures to determine "low performance," which takes us back to the perils of Chapter One. The interesting thing about operating an internal compliance organization in a public accounting firm was that we managed pretty successfully to operate as a hybrid between the client service model and the typical corporate model. Client service in large public accounting firms and consultancies is famously "up or out" – you are either promoted to the next level or fired. Corporate back office tends more towards "stay in your role until the person above you dies." I think we benefited from being able to promote people fairly regularly, although much less quickly than in client service, while not being forced to fire those who were perfectly good at their current jobs. While the organization was certainly not perfect, it was widely acknowledged to have a healthy culture of collaboration.

The more the governance of any organization is "for the people, by the people, and of the people," the less likely it is to be corrupted by jealousy and selfishness. As Tocqueville notes:

---

[122] 17 CFR Parts 229, 232, 240, 270, and 274, *Listing Standards for Erroneously Awarded Compensation,* 2022.

> *In the United States, those responsible for public affairs are often inferior in capability and in moral standards to those men aristocracy would bring to power, but their interests are mingled and identified with those of the majority of their fellow citizens…. In the United States, where public officials promote no class interests, the general and continuous course of government is beneficial even though the rulers are often incompetent and sometimes despicable.*[123]

Or more briefly:

> *It is not the elected official who produces the prosperity of American democracy but the fact that the official is elected.*[124]

I'm not suggesting popular elections for corporate CEOs. But some level of representation would surely be helpful. Germany's workers councils or private sector unions make running a company more cumbersome, but can introduce an important mechanism to make sure everyone is heard, not just those at the top. Some societies went so far as to have elaborate systems of periodic wealth redistribution, like the potlatch among the tribes of the North American Pacific Northwest where hosts would demonstrate their wealth and power by giving away goods.[125]

---

[123] De Tocqueville, *Democracy in America,* "What Are the Real Advantages Derived by American Society from Democratic Government."

[124] De Tocqueville, *Democracy in America*, "How Americans Combat the Effects of Individualism by Free Institutions."

[125] "Potlatch," Wikimedia Foundation, last modified October 27, 2024, https://en.wikipedia.org/wiki/Potlatch.

Finally, leaders need oversight just like everyone else. King David had the prophet Nathan to call him out when he behaved badly.[126] The United States government was designed with an explicit separation between the executive, legislative, and judiciary branches. CEOs benefit from a strong board of directors as a balance on their power. As the saying goes, governance doesn't matter... until it does. While checks and balances can and do slow things down, they mitigate issues like jealousy, tyranny, and CEOs asking for $50 billion dollar paychecks.[127] As Arthur Levitt noted when he was the chairman of the SEC:

> *In many respects, the discussion of effective corporate governance is more a cultural one than a programmatic one: Does a company expect its board to ask the tough questions and reject easy answers? Does it expect the board to challenge management? Does it expect its audit committee to consider the quality of the work and the independence of the auditor?*[128]

While I never achieved the level of king or CEO, when I was leading a function I benefited from a strong team that argued with me. In particular, I found over the years that a couple of the people who most regularly pushed back on me were very frequently right when we disagreed. It was always respectful and collegial, and it was the best kind of working environment. They felt able to safely express their views, and I benefited enormously from their different perspectives. Sometimes I benefited the most not when I took their advice, but when I didn't and later realized they had been right – something that got me a little closer to the elusive goal of humility.

---

[126] 2 Samuel 16.
[127] Wilmot, Stephen, "Tesla and Elon Musk Show Why Governance Doesn't Matter—Until It Does," *The Wall Street Journal,* February 16, 2024.
[128] Levitt, Arthur, SEC Chairman, *Remarks Before the Conference on the Rise and Effectiveness of New Corporate Governance Standards*, December 12, 2000, **https://www.sec.gov/news/speech/spch449.htm**.

It may be tempting to reach automatically for regulation to limit the power of business leaders. Of course, regulators themselves may be ambitious, especially if powerful, but as James Madison said, "Ambition must be made to counteract ambition."[129] A powerful regulator could be a useful balance against a powerful industry – and in some cases, indeed a necessary one. I don't particularly subscribe to the notion that regulators are unaccountable. Every regulatory staff member is ultimately accountable to a commissioner, who is accountable to political masters. Those hierarchies create their own incentives for power-seeking and self-protection, but they are not "unaccountable."

However, regulators are not accountable to the market. A company that doesn't serve its customers should (in a properly functioning market) be replaced by one that does. On the other hand, a regulatory agency is fundamentally a bureaucracy, which has a self-reinforcing stubbornness to it – as we'll discuss in Chapter Four. In addition, while regulators are likely to have a strong sense of mission, we've seen in the previous chapter that may be misused to justify bullying behavior. It's also reasonable to suspect that regulators may be jealous of the compensation earned by the executives of entities they regulate.

Even well-designed regulation by a good regulator can have unintended consequences. Robert Conway served as an audit partner in a Big Four public accounting firm, and then as an inspector for the Public Company Accounting Oversight Board (PCAOB) that regulates the profession. While he concluded that the PCAOB led to improvements in audit quality, he expressed concerns about some of its focus areas and its potential negative impact on retention in the profession. In some ways, it may have inadvertently worked against certain of its desired goals:

> *My overarching concern is that the PCAOB's inability to deliver cost-effective solutions to compliance in low risk areas has only fueled a further lack of auditor trust with respect to fees and scope and a diminished perception of audit value.*[130]

---

[129] Madison, *The Federalist Papers*, Federalist 51, 1788.
[130] Conway, Robert, *The Truth About Public Accounting* (2020), "The PCAOB's Erosion of Auditor-Client Trust."

Regulation may well be helpful and necessary in some cases, but I would not look to it as the ultimate safeguard. After all, as Juvenal said, "Who will guard the guardians?"[131] A regulatory authority needs to be subject to the same constraints as any other organization, including a clearly defined, limited scope of control, with proper accountability. Even in cases where there is clear bad behavior by a business, regulators or prosecutors may go too far in response. In the field of public accounting, for example, the U.S. government's conviction of Arthur Andersen for obstruction in the Enron scandal was overturned by a unanimous Supreme Court decision,[132] and charges against thirteen KPMG tax partners for allegedly participating in abusive tax shelters were dismissed for overreach by prosecutors that "shocked the conscience."[133] Of course by the time the Supreme Court ruled in the Andersen case, it was too late. One of the five largest public accounting firms in the world had been destroyed forever.

Regulatory oversight can help keep companies on the straight-and-narrow. However, if regulatory overreach induces terror, it may actually be counterproductive as we'll discuss in the next chapter.

In addition, regulators will always be playing catch-up to the companies they regulate. Regulators face the challenge that to be fair, they need to put in place limited, well-defined rules. But for the rules to be effective, the regulated entity has to actually be trying to comply and not slide around the edges. As Brennan notes:

> *External compliance regulations just don't – they're very hard to enforce, they're not very effective. It's way harder. I think it requires people who are in leadership positions to say, "We know this doesn't work, and now that I'm in charge, we're not doing it anymore. We're going to change the culture." And then they make a big deal out of it."*[134]

---

[131] Juvenal, *Satires*, Satire VI, trans. G.G. Ramsay (Digireads.com Publishing, 2020), original text 2nd Century. Ramsay translates the quote as "who wards the warders," but I've used the more common phrasing. Also, notwithstanding the usual sociopolitical interpretation of the phrase, it's worth noting that Satire VI was a pretty raunchy commentary on adultery.
[132] Arther Andersen LLP v. United States, 2005.
[133] Stein, Jeffrey, et al. v. United States, 2007.
[134] Sikand, Jay, *Dangerously Good #14*, "Revamped Voting & Managing Flawed People: Jason Brennan," 2021.

Regulators can encourage a strong tone at the top, as the PCAOB has recently done. Chair Erica Williams has rightly observed that "Firms' leadership and governance have a direct impact on their incentives and ability to provide high quality audit services investors deserve. Tone at the top and the priorities of firms' leadership strongly influence the level of commitment to audit quality."[135] But while it is possible in theory to regulate and test culture,[136] I tend to agree with Brennan in practice – culture must come from within, from the sense of mission. And from leaders and regulators who set the right tone, but give their teams the freedom to execute.

Like selfishness, jealousy will always be with us because we're wired that way. I suspect *Game of Thrones* was so popular not because of the sex and dragons (at least not entirely), but because it's a timeless story of jealous people behaving badly in a desperate quest for power. It's as good an illustration as any of what happens when you have a winner-takes-all struggle for absolute power. Limiting the stakes – money, power, what have you – is an important way to mitigate the problem of jealousy. But we need to bear in mind that the problem can only be mitigated, not solved. As James Madison says, "The inference to which we are brought is, that the causes of faction cannot be removed, and that relief is only to be sought in the means of controlling its effects."[137]

---

[135] Williams, Erica, PCAOB Chair, Statement on April 9, 2024, "Chair Williams Statement on Firm Reporting Proposal," https://pcaobus.org/news-events/speeches/speech-detail/chair-williams--statement-on-firm-reporting-proposal.

[136] PCAOB Spotlight, "Staff Priorities for 2024 Inspections and Interactions with Audit Committees," December 2023, https://assets.pcaobus.org/pcaob-dev/docs/default-source/documents/2024-priorities-spotlight.pdf?sfvrsn=7c595fae_4.

[137] Madison, *The Federalist Papers*, Federalist 10, 1788.

III. Shortsighted

"All human toil is for the mouth, yet the appetite is never satisfied."

- Ecclesiastes 6:7

One of the stories that I find oddest in Genesis is the competition between Isaac's twin sons, Esau and Jacob. These are the grandchildren of Abraham, the patriarch for whom the Abrahamic religions (Judaism, Christianity, and Islam) are named. Jacob, the second-born twin, goes on to become the father of the twelve tribes of Israel. He does so by trading Esau his birthright as firstborn for a bowl of lentil stew.

One day Esau was out hunting and didn't catch anything. He returned to camp hungry and asked for a bowl of the stew Jacob had made. Jacob let him have it, but only in exchange for his birthright. Esau said, "I am on the point of dying. What good is the right as firstborn to me?"[138] And so Esau exchanged the eternal blessing of God on all his descendants for a bowl of beans.

It's hard to understand Jacob's behavior, which seems less than honorable. However, I think the focus is intended to be not on Jacob, but on Esau. He lost all sight of the future because his stomach was rumbling. The New Testament supports that interpretation of the story: "See to it that no one becomes like Esau, an immoral and godless person, who sold his birthright for a single meal."[139]

Neurobiology gives Esau an explanation, if not exactly an excuse.

The "lizard brain" in humans (the brain stem, cerebellum, and basal ganglia) can override the higher brain functions of the cerebral cortex. That's by design. Max Bazerman explains the phenomenon of "ethical fading," or putting your moral reasoning in the back seat, as follows:

---

[138] Genesis 25:32.
[139] Hebrews 12:16.

Our body's innate needs may be partly to blame. Visceral responses dominate at the time we make decisions. Such mechanisms are hardwired into our brains to increase our chances of survival.[140]

If our ancestors' reaction to seeing what might be a tiger had been to contemplate the situation rather than run away, they would have gotten eaten. Imagine the following two reactions:

Ogg: "Hmm. There's a movement in the tall grass. It could perhaps be produced by the wind, or by a predator, or by a smaller animal generating a disproportionately large disturbance. Now, I believe the visual pattern I see over a length of at least six feet is not consistent with the tall grass itself, but rather appears to be the camouflage markings of an animal. Both carnivores and herbivores could profit from camouflage, so that fact is not determinative *per se* as to the level of risk. I suppose I should weigh the pros and cons of expending energy in the face of what may or may not prove to be a threat…"

Ugg: "Run away!"

Guess whether Ogg or Ugg lived to reproduce.

---

[140] Bazerman and Tenbrunsel, *Blind Spots*, "Why You Aren't as Ethical as You Think You Are."

What makes things interesting is that biological evolution lags social change. Timur Kuran points out that "it has been about 500 generations since the rise of agriculture – by evolutionary standards far too short a span for fundamental psychological readaptation."[141] All kinds of gut-level responses may not be adaptive anymore. Steven Pinker states that, "Human vice is proof that biological adaptation is, speaking literally, a thing of the past."[142] For example, in modern Western society, stuffing your face with all the sugar and fat you can lay hands on is a bad idea, because bulk calories are readily available and starvation is not a realistic threat for most of us. Similarly, men trying to have sex with every woman in sight is a lot less adaptive now than it probably was twenty thousand years ago. But people still eat things they shouldn't eat – unless you think that bacon double cheeseburger with a 32 ounce Coke is actually good for you. And people still cheat on their spouses, and watch pornography (which is a really weird hijacking of human neurotransmitters, since it's basically the equivalent of deliberately salivating over pictures of that bacon double cheeseburger). And people binge watch dumb shows on Netflix and doom scroll through Instagram.[143] And so forth.

The selfishness and jealousy of the first two chapters are relatively "high-functioning sins," as it were. They involve planning and scheming for advancement. Shortsightedness, by definition, does not. It is inherently counterproductive in the long term, driven by animal instinct in defiance of reason. The sins in question – gluttony, lust, sloth – tend to be things that animals like doing – eating, having sex, sleeping.

Shortsightedness is the last characteristic in this book that comes from Genesis; stubbornness and ingratitude are better exemplified in Exodus. As we wrap up the characteristics from Genesis, it may be helpful to reflect on the first three chapters together. The Catholic Church states that vices come from the devil, the world, and the flesh. When I teach catechism, I classify the seven deadly sins into a pyramid from the "lowest level" sins to the "highest level." We can use much the same groupings with the obnoxious behaviors of selfishness, jealousy, and shortsightedness.

---

[141] Kuran, Timur, *Private Truths, Public Lies* (Harvard University Press, 1995), "Private and Public Preferences."
[142] Pinker, *How the Mind Works*, "Revenge of the Nerds."
[143] Those references probably won't age well given how quickly technology platforms get replaced these days. You know what I mean.

That pyramid would look something like this:

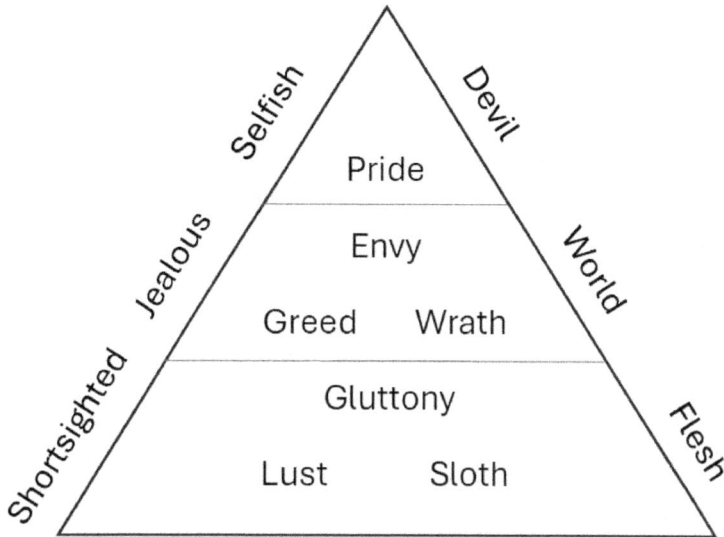

Christianity associates the sin of selfishness, or pride, with the devil. Per Milton, the devil's original sin, transmitted to humans in Eden, was insisting on getting his own way: "Better to reign in Hell than to serve in Heaven."[144] Adam and Eve were forced out of paradise because they wanted to be gods.

Jealousy, or the sins of the world, involves our hierarchical desire to be superior to other people. Cain couldn't stand the fact that God favored Abel more than him, and killed his brother for it.

Shortsightedness, or the sins of the flesh, comes from our basic animal instincts – hunger, lust, laziness.

---

[144] Milton, John, *Paradise Lost*, 1667, Book One.

As in our tiger example above, those animal instincts don't just involve seeking pleasure. They also involve avoiding danger. And because humans are social animals, danger means not just physical danger, but also social danger. The two may well have been closely related at some point – to be cast out of the group in ancient times could mean starvation, or being left defenseless to be eaten by that tiger after it finished digesting Ogg. These days social rejection isn't likely to mean death, although in wartime being deeply unpopular might directly curtail your chances of survival – see the Wikipedia entry for the term "fragging."

Yet even when there is no obvious physical threat, our neural wiring leaves us very attuned to social threat. I can personally attest to that. I purchased an Oura ring, which tracks all sorts of physiological responses. I mostly bought it to see if my snoring means that I have bad sleep apnea, which it turns out I don't – so it won't kill me, unless my wife smothers me to shut me up. However, I was able to use the ring to observe a number of other interesting things. For example, when I was being questioned by lawyers for four hours on a regulatory issue, my heart rate stayed consistently above 110 beats per minute the whole time, which is higher than it normally goes when I exercise, even though I was just sitting in a chair. Robert Wright explains the physiological effect:

> *The biochemical essence of the panic probably goes back to our reptilian days. Yet it was triggered not by its primordial trigger – threat to life and limb – but rather by a threat to status, a concern more characteristic of our primate days.*[145]

And Jonathan Haidt discusses the psychology behind it:

> *Our evolutionary advantage came from our larger brains and our capacity to form strong social groups, thus making us particularly attuned to social threats such as being shunned or shamed. People – and particularly adolescents – are often more concerned about the threat of "social death" than physical death.*

---

[145] Wright, *The Moral Animal*, "Darwin's Triumph."

Emotionally, anxiety is experienced as dread, worry, and, after a while, exhaustion. Cognitively, it becomes difficult to think clearly.[146]

I'll come back to the difficulty in thinking clearly under stress. But it ties back to Esau, his birthright, and that bowl of beans.

~~~

In a compliance organization, the sin of gluttony doesn't come up often. I can't recall ever seeing an ethics complaint against someone for eating too much. Lust makes an appearance sometimes. Sexual harassment is one of the easiest ways to get yourself fired these days. And there are more spectacular ways to mess up, like a former colleague who ordered a big box of pornographic materials to be sent to the office (presumably because he didn't want them delivered to his home where his wife might see them). Or you could sleep with your audit client, which, while not explicitly listed as such in the AICPA or SEC independence standards, is a no-no.

The sin that really comes up a lot in a compliance organization, though, is sloth. People can't be bothered to fill out the checklist we want them to. Or they don't take the time to do it right. A lot of that often turns out to be the organization's fault – we don't do a good job of explaining why the checklist matters. Or we don't make it easy to fill out. Both of those failures violate the "real rules" criteria from the first chapter, and suggest that the checklists fall into the category of "fake rules."

It can be hard to explain why someone has to fill out a long checklist to address what might possibly create a regulatory problem, or a conflict of interest, or a lawsuit. And it can be quite expensive to invest in the systems and processes to make the checklists work better by integrating all the different data sources. Tying compliance into the organization's mission is more promising, but takes a concerted focus from leadership. So the usual response of a compliance organization when people don't comply with our rules is to **YELL LOUDER**. Messages start to go out with phrases like **"YOU MAY NOW BE NONCOMPLIANT AND THERE WILL BE CONSEQUENCES."** Oddly, that doesn't tend to improve the results the way we'd expect it to. (No, I'm not being sarcastic – at least not much.)

---

[146] Haidt, Jonathan, *The Anxious Generation* (Penguin Press, 2024), "The Surge of Suffering."

Being in charge of several compliance organizations, I started to think about why yelling louder didn't work. I reflected on my experience with my third son, who has high-functioning autism spectrum disorder. I sometimes get very frustrated when I'm trying to get him to pay attention to a task and he doesn't. It's not that he's being deliberately obstructive or negligent. He's one of the nicest, most helpful people I know. He just has trouble focusing on something that doesn't interest him. I was the same way as a teenager, and to some extent I still am. I'm often bad at getting him to engage, in spite of the fact (or perhaps because of the fact) that I'm probably mildly autistic myself. It seems like sometimes he doesn't engage at all with the task until I yell at him, and when I do that, he panics, and doesn't engage productively.

As it turns out, there's a graph for that. The Yerkes-Dodson Law, a psychological construct dating to 1908,[147] shows that performance on a difficult task is poor under conditions of both low arousal **and** high arousal. And yes, this is a graph with performance on one axis and arousal on the other and it's not about sex. When I presented this graph to my compliance team there was a lot of giggling, mostly from my female colleagues. I was a little surprised to learn that I wasn't the most immature person in the room.[148]

---

[147] Yerkes, Robert and John Dodson, "The relation of strength of stimulus to rapidity of habit-formation," *Journal of Comparative Neurology and Psychology, 18*, 1908. The graph shown here is edited to omit the curve showing that for simple tasks, performance does not drop at higher arousal states, because advanced cognition isn't required. The graph is sourced from Wikimedia Foundation, "Hebbian version of the Yerkes-Dodson law," **https://en.wikipedia.org/wiki/Yerkes%E2%80%93Dodson_law#/media/File:HebbianYerkesDodson. svg**
[148] I suppose the graph works for sex too, at least for men, since… oh, never mind. Maybe I am the most immature person in the room.

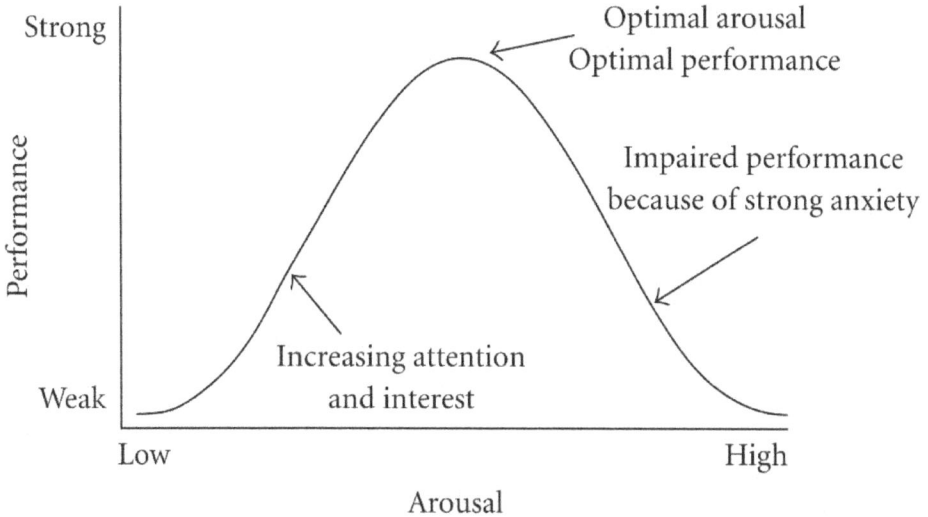

"Arousal" in this case refers to engagement, or stress. The results are perhaps not surprising. If you don't care about the task you do poorly, because you don't care. If you are extremely stressed about the task you do poorly, because your neurotransmitters have been hijacked by your lizard brain's anxiety. Recall Haidt's observation above, "Cognitively, it becomes difficult to think clearly." When Esau was hungry, the higher brain functions required to think about God's eternal blessing on his descendants went straight out the window. The same thing would have happened if he'd been under social stress.

When we try to get people to "do the right thing," we often flip them straight from "don't care" to "panicked." Messages declaring "**YOU MAY NOW BE OUT OF COMPLIANCE AND THERE WILL BE CONSEQUENCES**" skip straight over the optimal arousal and performance part of the curve. Instead, the person we want to comply goes straight from low arousal to high arousal, and performance stays bad. That's what tended to happen with my son. My wife is much better than I am at increasing his attention and interest to get optimal performance.[149]

~~~

I don't believe there are any easy ways to counter the biological basis of shortsightedness. Our neurological wiring makes it very hard to employ the rational part of the brain when our emotions are engaged. Jonathan Haidt uses the metaphor of the "elephant and rider" – our rational mind is the rider, while our emotions are the elephant.[150] Haidt deliberately rejected the Platonic notion of horses controlled by a rational charioteer,[151] because he believes the emotional elephant is much stronger than the rational rider. The rider can turn the elephant, but only if the elephant isn't all riled up. If the elephant really wants to go in a particular direction, it's going to go in that direction. As Alinsky says, "In this world irrationality clings to man like his shadow so that the right things are done for the wrong reasons – afterwards, we dredge up the right reasons for justification."[152]

Bazerman explains this irrationality, reflected in Saint Paul's complaint about his own behavior from the Introduction, as the difference between the "want self" and the "should self":

---

[149] I have a hypothesis that people with autism spectrum disorder have a narrower than average range of optimal performance on the Yerkes-Dodson curve, with much more of their experience lying in the tails. Many things either don't engage their interest at all, or produce so much stress that they can't respond effectively. I also hypothesize that modern online technology (social media, pornography, video games, short videos) is very precisely targeted at the "optimal engagement" part of the curve. I further believe exposure to that technology makes it harder for everyone (but especially individuals with autism spectrum disorder) to constructively engage with things that are outside the "sweet spot" on the curve, i.e., either boring or stressful, because the technology narrows our range of effective response. I haven't seen research on those hypotheses, but I think that analysis is worth undertaking.

[150] Haidt, *The Righteous Mind*, "The Intuitive Dog and Its Rational Tail."

[151] Plato, *Phaedrus*, trans. Benjamin Jowett, 4th Century BC.

[152] Alinsky, *Rules for Radicals*, "The Purpose."

The want self describes the side of you that's emotional, affective, impulsive, and hot-headed. In contrast, your should self is rational, cognitive, thoughtful, and cool-headed... The should self dominates before and after we make a decision, but the want self often wins at the moment of decision.[153]

The "should self" is Haidt's rational rider, the "want self" is the much stronger emotional elephant. I believe what that means for organizational design is that we need to be very deliberate in how we engage the emotions. If an appeal to "do the right thing" has no emotional resonance, it gets ignored in favor of things that do resonate. Those things that do resonate might be following "real rules" around revenue and profitability, or they might be random "shiny objects" that attract people's attention more than completing a compliance exercise. Shiny objects might be eating a bacon double cheeseburger or binge-watching Netflix – anything that engages the shortsighted animal part of the brain rather than the rational part.

I strongly suspect that the algorithms used to engage our attention online are only making it harder to resist the shiny objects. From a psychological perspective, sources ranging from Jonathan Haidt's *The Anxious Generation* to Jeff Orlowski's docudrama *The Social Dilemma* report extensively on how social media is designed to hijack neurotransmitters and keep us engaged with those shiny objects. Or as I tell my catechism students, it used to at least take some effort to commit most of the deadly sins, and it was challenging to commit more than one at the same time. These days you can sit in your bed munching Doritos while writing a hateful tweet about someone who condemns the kind of porn you like to watch.

---

[153] Bazerman and Tenbrunsel, *Blind Spots*, "Why You Aren't as Ethical as You Think You Are."

Getting someone's attention requires engaging the emotions and pulling them away from the shiny objects. On the other hand, if the appeal to "do the right thing" is framed too aggressively in terms of consequences, the brain does indeed engage – but as the Yerkes-Dodson curve shows, it engages in an unproductive way. People may panic and behave ineffectively. If the task is sufficiently complex and people come to believe they can't succeed, the panic may even lead to learned helplessness, the phenomenon where individuals conclude they can't succeed at a task and stop trying.[154] Again, as Haidt stated, "Emotionally, anxiety is experienced as dread, worry, and, after a while, exhaustion."

The Dalai Lama observed that "the basic or underlying nature of human beings is gentleness" and that "feelings of frustration, fear, agitation, and anger can be destructive to our health."[155] I agree with that view, with the caveat that gentleness belongs to the "should self." Unfortunately, in practice the "want self" very often engages in exactly the frustrated, fearful, agitated, angry, self-destructive behavior that the Dalai Lama warns against. [156] Indeed, he notes that "responding to a trying situation with patience and tolerance rather than anger and hatred involves active restraint, which comes from a strong, self-disciplined mind."[157]

---

[154] Originally documented by Martin Seligman in research on dogs and subsequently extended to humans. Seligman, Martin and Steven Maier, "Failure to escape traumatic shock," *Journal of Experimental Psychology, 74(1)*, 1967.

[155] HH Dalai Lama and Cutler, *The Art of Happiness*, "Reclaiming Our Innate State of Happiness."

[156] That is not unique to humans. Our nearest relatives, chimpanzees, are aggressive, exploitative, murderous, and warlike. See for example Sandel, Aaron and David Watts, "Lethal Coalitionary Aggression Associated with a Community Fission in Chimpanzees (Pan troglodytes) at Ngogo, Kibale National Park, Uganda," *International Journal of Primatology*, February 2021.

[157] HH Dalai Lama and Cutler, *The Art of Happiness*, "Bring About Change."

I observed stress and emotional exhaustion working in a counterintuitive way in the same sell-side diligence project I mentioned in Chapter Two. I worked with the client's financial planning and analysis ("FP&A") group to pull together numbers for potential buyers. Of course, the FP&A team was worried that they might lose their jobs in the transaction, since mergers and acquisitions often target cost savings by consolidating headcount. But rather than working hard to demonstrate their usefulness, the FP&A team lapsed into hopelessness and despair, and getting anything out of them was like pulling teeth. It wasn't a rational response – but it was a very human one.[158]

One way of thinking about the proper balance of engagement is that an organization needs to both "demand" and "deserve" that people do the right thing.

The "demand" side is obvious, and tends to be (poorly) expressed by yelling louder. To be effective, the "demand" side needs to constructively engage the emotions – explain why the task is important in a way that resonates. You have to move the population to the right on the Yerkes-Dodson curve, out of indifference, but without pushing them into panic.

The "deserve" side is less obvious, and recalls the fourth characteristic of "real rules" from Chapter One – systems and processes must make the rules easy to follow. It's all very well to tell people what they need to do. If they don't have the time or tools to effectively execute those tasks, bad things happen. They lose whatever motivation they had gained from a well-articulated "demand." They may begin to believe you don't really mean what you said – if you did, you would have made it easier to comply. And they may even sink into learned helplessness, concluding they can't get it right so there's no sense in trying.

The following techniques can help overcome shortsightedness and help people do the right thing:

(1) Engage the emotions in a positive rather than punitive way;

(2) Use input and feedback to test the resonance of messaging;

---

[158] It doesn't always go that way. Early in my career I audited a municipal water utility. The utility had undertaken a massive, and massively unsuccessful, project to rebuild the municipal storm sewer system. One day I arrived to find that the entire engineering department had been fired. The accounting department was very cooperative after that.

(3) Limit compliance tasks to the essential; and

(4) Give people the tools to achieve compliance.

Scaring people is always an easy way to get their attention. And sometimes it's a necessary way. We all slow down when we drive by a police car. It's well understood that in most contexts, removing enforcement will lead to increasing non-compliance. Dictatorships of the right and left have both tended to enjoy low crime rates. But that kind of terror goes too far. As Tacitus said of the Roman Empire, "they make a desert and call it peace."[159]

Humans are to a large extent rationally self-interested, after all, so there's a role for fear. But hopefully none of us aspire to rule by terror, or participate in an organization ruled by terror. Both because that's unpleasant, and because as we saw with the Yerkes-Dodson curve, it doesn't actually produce great outcomes. While we slow down, how many of us are at our best driving on the highway with that police car behind us? As Tocqueville says of using terror to achieve compliance:

> *In the Middle Ages when it was difficult to catch criminals, whenever judges did seize a few, they often inflicted awful punishments on these wretched people, which did not reduce the number of the guilty. It has since been discovered that by making justice both more certain and milder, it becomes at the same time more effective.[160]*

Ibn Khaldun is even more forceful in his view that governing through fear is actively counterproductive:

---

[159] Tacitus, Publius Cornelius, *The Complete Works of Tacitus* (Digireads.com Publishing, 2013), original text 2nd Century, "Agricola." The phrase is attributed to Calgacus, a Scottish warlord, who was fighting against Agricola, Tacitus' father-in-law. The translation of Tacitus in my library renders the phrase as, "where they make a desert, they call it peace," but I've used the more common phrasing.
[160] De Tocqueville, *Democracy in America*, "Judicial Power in the United States and its Effects Upon Political Society."

Good rulership is equivalent to mildness. If the ruler uses force and is ready to mete out punishment and eager to expose the faults of people and to count their sins, his subjects become fearful and depressed and seek to protect themselves against him through lies, ruses, and deceit. This becomes a character trait of theirs. Their mind and character become corrupted.[161]

Ibn Khaldun obviously did not believe in lawlessness any more than Tocqueville did. But he noted that:

Clearly, then, governmental and educational laws destroy fortitude, because their restraining influence is something that comes from outside. The religious laws, on the other hand, do not destroy fortitude, because their restraining influence is something inherent.[162]

To generalize from Ibn Khaldun's two statements, I believe his point is that rules that are imposed by force sap the will of the group and may actually produce worse behavior. Effective rules have to come from an appeal to something greater. As a devout Muslim, Ibn Khaldun's locus of that appeal was religion. More broadly, we can call that "mission."

I agree that it is more effective to move people to the center of the Yerkes-Dodson curve by engaging them emotionally with the mission. A simple example is the use of "X days since last accident" signs. The visible sign helps everyone recall that safety is important, while setting the positive goal of increasing the "days since." Of course, there will likely need to be punishments for extreme forms of non-compliance. Some small number of people will deliberately do bad things. Others may be perfectly good people, but poorly suited to the organization because their values don't align well with its values. Those people may need to either be educated or counseled out of the organization. But the application of terror, while effective against an enemy in war, doesn't build a cohesive team.

---

[161] Ibn Khaldun, *The Muqaddimah*, Ch.3.
[162] Ibid, Ch.2.

Of course, mission-driven appeals to positive emotions are harder to execute than fear-driven appeals to negative emotions. Negative emotions have a special resonance for us – that's why so many successful politicians stoke fear and anger. Humans are generally wired to respond more urgently to threats than rewards. Haidt discusses "discover vs. defend mode," giving the example of what happens when early humans find cherries (discovery) but are then confronted with a leopard (defense):

> *The behavioral inhibition system (BIS), in contrast, turns on when threats are detected, such as hearing a leopard roar nearby as you're picking those cherries. You all stop what you are doing. Appetite is suppressed as your bodies flood with stress hormones and your thinking turns entirely to identifying the threat and finding ways to escape it.*[163]

But as Haidt points out when he discusses the inhibiting effect of fear on cognition, and the Yerkes-Dodson curve demonstrates, if you want the best thinking from your people, you need to motivate with positive emotions rather than punish with negative ones. The stress hormones are great at producing a fight-or-flight response; they're bad at engaging the higher brain functions.

Getting those emotional appeals right takes time, effort, and iteration. As the next chapter will discuss in more detail, user feedback is necessary to figure out how to appeal to people's better natures. Or as I tended to put it to my teams, "fish using the bait the fish like, not the bait you like."

I had that driven home pretty forcefully when I was redesigning an intranet site. We were updating content, and I also wanted to make a major change to how the information was organized. Historically, we'd arranged the content based on our service delivery lifecycle. That didn't make a lot of intellectual sense to me. I told my team we should arrange it around subject matter area instead – confidentiality, objectivity, and so forth, using the framework set out in the AICPA Code of Ethics. No one on the team agreed with me, so I asked the team to mock up two versions and run them by our client serving professionals. None of the client servers liked my version either. We went with the original structure.

---

[163] Haidt, *The Anxious Generation*, "Discover Mode and the Need for Risky Play."

Not only do discussion and dissent allow the best ideas to bubble to the top, they also promote buy-in and good organizational hygiene. That helps keep people in the right spot on the Yerkes-Dodson curve – engaged but not frightened. As Haidt notes:

> *Psychological safety is among the best indicators of a healthy workplace culture. But in a psychologically safe group, members can disagree with each other and criticize each other's ideas respectfully.*[164]

Recall that appeals to get people to do the right thing have more competition than ever. Modern populations don't just need to contend with the temptation to do the wrong thing. They have to contend with the precisely targeted electronic distracters that specialize in keeping our neurotransmitters in the center of the Yerkes-Dodson curve – social media, online gaming, pornography, advertising, you name it.

In my experience compliance organizations are not good at using the tools of persuasion in which marketing organizations have so much expertise. It's fascinating to me that Cialdini consistently uses the term "compliance" to describe marketing appeals in his book on the psychology of persuasion.[165] But that correlation seems not to be widely understood in compliance organizations, which tend to rely instead on some form of yelling louder, including punishment. Of course, there's a difference between getting someone to buy a time-share and getting them to fill out a checklist. However, in each case, you are trying to get someone to do something they're not inclined to do. I believe compliance organizations could benefit considerably from using more of the emotional psychology of "compliance" as Cialdini defines it.[166]

---

[164] Ibid.

[165] Cialdini, *Influence.*

[166] I won't get into an in-depth discussion of Cialdini's findings. The book is well worth reading on its own, and many of the findings don't translate well to the kind of compliance I'm talking about. But some of them do. For example, in his chapter on *Weapons of Influence*, he notes that simply using the word "because" in a request considerably increases the chances of compliant behavior.

Of course, emotional appeals may resonate differently with different segments of the population. I found it was easier to drive compliance among CPAs than non-CPA professionals in a public accounting firm. That may have been because CPAs are generally more compliant, as suggested by Dan Ariely who found that accountants are the least creative of all professionals and therefore the most honest.[167] Or it might have been because the compliance matters in question had more intrinsic emotional resonance with CPAs. In either case, I found it was important to segment the population and craft specific interventions for those segments.

Of course, no discussion of compliance is complete without a discussion of one of the words most commonly associated with it, "bureaucracy." Ariely's latest venture is the sarcastically named Center for Advanced Bureaucracy.[168] He advances a couple of ideas. First, similar to Ibn Khaldun, he suggests that intrinsic motivation (mission) is better than extrinsic motivation (bureaucracy). Obviously I agree. Secondly and more significantly, he objects very strongly to the bureaucratization of life.

"Bureaucracy" is a bit of a tough word to define, at least as commonly used. Merriam-Webster defines it variously as:

> *1.a: a body of nonelected government officials*
>
> *1.b: an administrative policymaking group*
>
> *2: government characterized by specialization of functions, adherence to fixed rules, and a hierarchy of authority*
>
> **3: a system of administration marked by officialism, red tape, and proliferation**[169]

For Ariely's purposes and ours, we're focused on the third definition. Large organizations outside of government have what any reasonable outside observer would characterize as "bureaucracy." I used to be in charge of parts of it.

---

[167] Ariely, *The Honest Truth About Dishonesty*, "Creativity and Dishonesty." Ariely finds that individuals who are more creative are better able to justify their own dishonesty; therefore, people who are less creative are more honest.

[168] **https://centerforbureaucracy.com/**.

[169] **https://www.merriam-webster.com/dictionary/bureaucracy**.

I'm not as negative about bureaucracy as Ariely is. That might be due to my time serving in it – I probably had a different view before. In the next chapter I'll discuss my idea of bureaucracy as an immune system – why it exists, and where it can go wrong. But where Ariely and I certainly agree is that the number of rules needs to be sufficiently limited that people can be reasonably expected to know and follow them. As James Madison stated, "It will be of little avail to the people, that the laws are made by men of their own choice, if the laws be so voluminous that they cannot be read, or so incoherent that they cannot be understood."[170]

There's always the temptation to add one more rule, one more safeguard, one more control. If ten commandments are good, surely twenty would be better? Or at least some sub-paragraphs? Maybe fifteen commandments, each with five sub-parts? Tocqueville notes that, "The nature of absolute power in democratic times is not to be cruel or savage but minute and interfering."[171]

Excessive rulemaking doesn't just irritate the governed. I firmly believe it also makes the governance less effective. The problem with too many rules is twofold:

- Humans have limited processing capacity. We're shortsighted, after all. A lot of our time is going to be taken up with eating, sleeping, and watching Game of Thrones, not a diligent search for every possible rule we could comply with. Just because something is written down somewhere doesn't mean we can find it. While "ignorance of the law is no excuse,"[172] there comes a point where the rules become so voluminous and complex they cannot reasonably be complied with. For example, in *Cheek vs. United States*, the Supreme Court found that "A genuine, good faith belief that one is not violating the Federal tax law based on a misunderstanding caused by the complexity of the tax law (e.g., the complexity of the statute itself) is a defense to a charge of 'willfulness.'"[173]

---

[170] Madison, *The Federalist Papers*, Federalist 62, 1788.
[171] De Tocqueville, *Democracy in America*, "How in America the Taste for Physical Pleasures is Combined with Love of Freedom and Concern for Public Affairs."
[172] "Ignorantia juris non excusat" in Roman legal tradition; see also Leviticus 5:17.
[173] Cheek, 498 U.S. at 203.

- At some point the volume of rules actively creates resistance. Once compliance is perceived as bureaucracy, it loses any emotional force. No one gets excited about filling out a checklist. Attention and compliance drop like a rock. When I was recently opening a new IRA, I had to read over a hundred pages of boilerplate disclosures that theoretically warned me of significant risks; needless to say, despite being an auditor working in a compliance function, I didn't read the disclosures in any detail. Similarly, as my team was revisiting our engagement acceptance process, we learned through testing that one question was answered wrong about 80% of the time. Fortunately, those errors didn't produce any actual regulatory, legal, or quality risk. But they showed how layering on more and more checklist items actually made things worse rather than better.

Burdensome checklists bring us straight to the last remediation item in this section. Compliance needs to be made easy. Again, there are two reasons:

- The obvious reason is that people can more readily comply with an easy process. If buying a product on Amazon were as hard as registering to provide social security withholding for your household employee, no one would ever buy anything from them.[174] All successful companies in e-commerce (and for that matter regular commerce) make it as easy as possible to get a transaction completed. Compliance organizations may have the luxury of requiring people to do a task, but it doesn't mean that requirement should be difficult to execute on.

---

[174] The Social Security Administration is a pet peeve of mine. Because I am a pretty compliant person with a keen interest in ethics and keeping my CPA license in good standing, I pay taxes for the couple that spends two hours cleaning our house every two weeks. Signing up to do so required me to use a website, send an email, make a phone call, send a fax, and exchange physical "snail mail." The SSA process is the textbook example of how *not* to get people to do the right thing when it's something they probably don't want to do.

- Second and less obvious, but equally important, we return to the fourth characteristic of "real rules." They're easy to comply with. Again, people aren't stupid, and they frequently operate on inference. If we tell them that something is important but don't invest in making it easy, they will suspect that it's not important. If it were really important, we would have invested in making it easy. There may be perfectly valid reasons why that's not straightforward to do, but people are unlikely to appreciate them (remember, their attention is limited). Instead, they will likely conclude that something that isn't facilitated doesn't really matter.

Balancing "demand" and "deserve" is challenging. It's easy and tempting to conclude that when people aren't doing the right thing, it's because they're lazy at best, or malicious at worst. Strident demands or harsh punishments can seem like the right solutions, but aren't likely to drive the right level of engagement or long-term focus. Instead, anything that's important needs to be explained and enabled.

IV. Stubborn

"But many things that might work don't."

– Daniel Kahneman[175]

I always felt a little sorry for Pharaoh, despite the fact that he was an egomaniacal, murderous sociopath. It must have sucked to be a wannabe god-king stuck between his idiot sorcerers and the actual God. When Moses turned the waters of Egypt to blood, Pharaoh's sorcerers did the same with their magic. You have to imagine Pharaoh was thinking, "How about you turn the blood back to water instead of giving me more blood?" The sorcerers even tried to produce more gnats to match the third plague.[176]

But at some point, after the blood and gnats and frogs and flies and pestilence and boils and hail and locusts and darkness, before the death of the firstborn, you'd think Pharaoh would have given up and let the Hebrews go. The issue is confused a bit by God's statement that he "will make Pharaoh so headstrong that, despite the many signs and wonders that I work in the land of Egypt, Pharaoh will not listen to you."[177]

We don't need God to make us stubborn, though. We're stubborn all by ourselves. Giving it a nicer name, Cialdini dedicates an entire chapter of *Influence* to the potentially pathological aspects of consistency. He points out that consistency is generally prized as showing "personal and intellectual strength" while inconsistency "may be seen as indecisive, confused, two-faced." A further benefit is that once we've reached a conclusion, "we really don't have to think hard about the issue anymore."[178]

---

[175] Lewis-Kraus, Gideon, "They Studied Dishonesty. Was Their Work a Lie?"
[176] Exodus 7:20-22, 8:12-14.
[177] Exodus 7:3. Leon Kass in *Founding God's Nation* (Yale University Press, 2021), "The Contest With Egypt," postulates that Pharaoh must be as resolute as possible in resisting Moses in order to fully demonstrate that even the supreme ruler of the most powerful nation of the era (a nation that seeks to wholly control life from birth through death with technology and sorcery) is only a man, not a god.
[178] Cialdini, *Influence*, "Commitment and Consistency."

While Ralph Waldo Emerson felt that "a foolish consistency is the hobgoblin of little minds,"[179] changing your mind can make you appear weak. A leader can find it dangerous to their power. As Nietzsche put it:

> *Our adherents never forgive us if we take sides against ourselves: for in their eyes this means not only rejecting their love but also exposing their intelligence.*[180]

We'd rather be consistent than right, because changing our minds to be right would mean admitting that we'd originally been wrong.

It's common for humans, especially those with any degree of power or prestige, to believe that we know best. And once we decide that we know best, our natural inclination is to defend that opinion to the death – or at least far past the point of logic. Consistency then easily passes into stubbornness, where we believe that the very act of sticking to a position, whatever its merits, is a moral good. Have you ever found yourself in an argument, defending positions you don't really believe because you've followed yourself down a rabbit hole of consistency? Or agreeing to do something you didn't want to do, because it was consistent with something you'd previously agreed to? Cialdini describes how manipulators from salespeople to POW camp guards can weaponize consistency into a pathology by getting people to agree to one small thing, and then progressively building on that agreement against the target's own interests.

---

[179] Emerson, Ralph Waldo, *Self-Reliance and Other Essays* (Grapevine India, 2023), original text 1841, "Self-Reliance."
[180] Nietzsche, Friedrich, *Basic Writings of Nietzsche,* trans. Walter Kaufmann (The Modern Library, 2000), original text 1878, "Human, All Too Human."

Some amount of stubborn consistency is useful, and perhaps necessary. In the comedy *The Good Place*,[181] the moral philosophy professor Chidi is so indecisive, and considers every choice in such agonizing detail, that he is sent to hell for making everyone around him miserable. One of my closest friends – let's call him Jonah – could have been the model for Chidi. In one incident when we were in high school, Jonah and I were part of a triumvirate pushing the student counsel to impeach the freshman class officers, a radical and unprecedented act. The freshman class officers were grossly incompetent, and our plan was going swimmingly until the day of the vote, when Jonah stood up and delivered an impassioned defense of them, completely betraying me and my other friend. The impeachment carried anyway. When we confronted Jonah, he was deeply apologetic and said he had gotten caught up in the ethical complexity of the moment, and wished he had it all to do over again.

The impeachment generated the expected pushback from the freshman officers' parents. The freshman officers didn't care, which is why they were incompetent, but their parents wanted the officer role on their children's transcripts for college applications. The administration intervened and insisted that I, as the student counsel secretary, strike the impeachment from the minutes. I refused but offered the compromise that we would vote to reinstate. The vote to reinstate failed and the freshman officers remained impeached, except guess who gave another impassioned speech in favor of reinstatement? It's amazing Jonah has survived to reproduce. (He's actually a wonderful person and has largely gotten over his dithering.)

---

[181] Schur, *The Good Place*.

My friend was the very unusual case of someone who was not stubborn enough. That's not how I am, as you might guess from my refusal to do what my high school principal ordered me to do. I've fallen into that trap not just in my personal life but professionally as well. Over a decade ago my firm centralized the majority of our conflict checking process into a global shared services center. I disagreed with the decision, at least for the United States. I felt it would slow response times and lower the quality compared to our excellent on-shore team. I was just starting my role as the service line quality leader, and felt it was important to express my view. I shared my thoughts with my direct superior, the deputy vice chair for the service line in the U.S. He was inclined to agree. Emboldened, I presented my opinion to the U.S. vice chair. He listened, then told me that the decision had already been finalized and wouldn't be revisited. I insisted, setting out my logic more forcefully. He told me he would not expend political capital on reversing the decision. I said that he didn't need to fight the battle, that I would do it, but that I felt strongly.

The deputy vice chair, who was a friend, reached out and told me, "Disagree with the vice chair one more time and you'll be finding yourself a new job."

I'm stubborn by nature, I freely admit it. I'm often stubborn when it serves no particularly useful purpose. In college I wanted to minor in Spanish to reflect the fact that I'd learned to speak it and had taken advanced Spanish courses as electives. The College of Commerce[182] informed me that I couldn't minor outside the College. I escalated – I'd double-major. The College informed me I couldn't double-major outside the College. I asked what it would take to get academic recognition in Spanish. The College informed me the only way would be to withdraw from the College of Commerce, transfer to the College of Liberal Arts and Sciences, get a degree in Spanish, and petition the College of Commerce for a degree in Accountancy – which they would not be compelled to give me, since I wouldn't be part of the College. So I did that. Fortunately, the College of Commerce accepted my petition.

---

[182] These days it's the Gies College of Business.

So my natural reaction to the dispute with my boss was to be stubborn, even against my interests. I was inclined to push back again, whatever the consequences. I had recently converted to Catholicism, so praying for guidance seemed appropriate. I expected that if I got any divine inspiration, it would be something along the lines of sacrificing my personal economic interests in favor of what I thought was right. Instead I received the first and so far only direct message I've gotten from God. It was one word: "Submit."

It wasn't at all what I'd expected, and it took me a while to figure out what to make of it. Was God really telling me to just suck it up? Was that little voice not God at all, but just a subconscious survival instinct saying, "Don't get fired, idiot"?

In any case, I spent a lot of time thinking about that one word, "submit." I realized that what my boss wanted to do wasn't illegal, or immoral, or unethical. I just thought it was a dumb decision. I had explained to him why I thought it was a dumb decision, and he had disagreed. Maybe I was right, or maybe he was right. It didn't really matter. The judgment call was his to make, and at that point, I was just being stubborn. So I gave up and we centralized the conflict checking process. Ironically, several years later, I became the global conflicts leader, and had to convince other people to let me further centralize and standardize the global process. Like Marx said, "man's consciousness changes with every change in the conditions of his material existence, in his social relations and in his social life."[183] We're stubborn, until something happens that makes us change our minds.

And that, I believe, is where consistency crosses the line into pig-headedness. Think about what new facts would make you change your mind. For a deeply held moral belief, there might be none. But in most cases, new data should make us modify our views. In Pharaoh's case, when the annoying Jewish guy turned his staff into a snake, okay, Pharaoh's magicians could do that. The same with turning water into blood. But at some point well before the tenth plague, Pharaoh had enough data to change his mind. Unfortunately, for many people and processes, just like Pharaoh, learning new facts frequently isn't enough to make a difference.

~~~

---

[183] Marx and Engels, *The Communist Manifesto*, Ch.II.

I've encountered two distinct kinds of stubbornness in my career: individual stubbornness and organizational stubbornness. They're two sides of the same coin and they're frequently in conflict.

Individual stubbornness takes the form of extremism, whereas organizational stubbornness takes the form of bureaucracy. The first seeks to impose the individual's will over all objections, in the certainty that the individual is right. The second seeks to stop any individual from ever imposing their will on the system, in the certainty that the individual is wrong. Extremism is the progressive flavor of stubbornness, whereas bureaucracy is the conservative flavor.[184] What they have in common is an unwillingness to change in the face of evidence. I'll deal with them separately, and then try to tie them back together.

Extremism is the stubborn arrogance that comes from knowing you're right. Some degree of it is important to accomplish anything. As Saul Alinsky points out, it's hard to get anyone riled up to make a change if you say, "We're about 60% right, and the other side is about 40% right, and so our way is slightly better." I agree with him to a point. However, the risk is that by framing any debate in absolute black and white terms, we call for intellectual dishonesty in the service of the ultimate good.[185] From that absolutism comes necessarily the demonization of anyone who disagrees: "One acts decisively only in the conviction that all the angels are on one side and all the devils on the other."[186]

The problem is that, as we've established above, there aren't likely to be any angels or devils on either side. There are going to be a bunch of selfish, jealous, shortsighted, stubborn, ungrateful people on both sides. Extremism loses sight of that. As Robert F. Kennedy said:

---

[184] I'm going to use the term "progressive" to mean favoring change, and "conservative" to mean resisting change. Neither one in this usage has anything to do with a particular set of economic, social, or military policies. I'm going to leave the word "liberal" out of this discussion entirely, since it has historically meant many different things to many different people, and its use seems to be more muddled than ever today.

[185] Alinsky, *Rules for Radicals*, "Of Means and Ends."

[186] Ibid, "Tactics."

> *What is objectionable, what is dangerous about extremists is*
> *not that they are extreme, but that they are intolerant. The*
> *evil is not what they say about their cause, but what they say*
> *about their opponents.[187]*

The tactical use of extremism might make sense if we had an exceptionally high degree of confidence that we were right. My observation, however, is that even very smart people are frequently wrong about all kinds of things. When I was trying to strengthen a particular compliance program, I called in an eminent Harvard professor who is an expert on performance evaluation and incentives.[188] As he tried to understand the problem, he asked what we had done previously to address it. I described half a dozen interventions that we had tried, none of which had made much of a dent in the issue. At the end of that conversation he said, "You'd really think those would have worked."

As Daniel Kahneman said in this chapter's opening quote, "many things that might work don't." In fact, what improved compliance significantly was a requirement I had nearly rejected as burdensome, annoying, and probably unhelpful. We did it anyway because we felt a need to try everything. And it indeed proved to be burdensome and annoying; it also proved to be the only intervention that made any difference.

Edmund Burke set out the view that no one individual, no matter how brilliant, can have that exceptionally high degree of confidence in always being right.

> *We are afraid to put men to live and trade each on his own*
> *private stock of reason, because we suspect that this stock in*
> *each man is small, and that the individuals would do better*
> *to avail themselves of the general bank and capital of*
> *nations and of ages.[189]*

Alinsky himself acknowledged the risk of arrogance:

---

[187] Kennedy, Robert, *The Pursuit of Justice* (Ishi Press International, 2017), original text 1964, "Extremism, Left and Right."
[188] This was the case where I almost recruited Dr. Francesca Gino.
[189] Burke, Edmund, *Reflections on the Revolution in France* (Digireads.com Publishing, 2009), original text 1790.

But it is equally difficult for you to surrender that little image of God created in our own likeness, which lurks in all of us and tells us that we secretly believe we know what's best for the people.[190]

Alinksy was very much a realist, but also very much a progressive. He believed that the arc of change more or less inevitably bent towards the positive. The problem is that some social and economic experiments play out on a long time scale. Boeing's focus on cost-cutting worked really well for a while – until it didn't. There is a reason why traditions and bureaucracy exist as a brake on change.

I've often characterized bureaucracy as a kind of immune system for the organization, which is a perspective I could only find articulated by one other person, Colonel Bill DeMarco. Colonel DeMarco states that "the 'bureaucratic immune system' responds with initial resistance to anything that might disturb the status quo."[191] I agree. Where we differ is that I don't think that's **necessarily** a bad thing.

Humans have an immune system for a reason. New microorganisms entering your body are probably bad. Maybe a genetic mutation is going to give you the ability to shoot lasers out of your eyes – but it's probably just going to give you cancer. That's why T-cells kill mutations.

---

[190] Alinsky, *Rules for Radicals*, "In the Beginning."
[191] Demarco, Bill, "Public Sector Intrapreneurship: Overcoming Bureaucratic Immune Systems," *Cambridge Social Innovation Blog*, October 20, 2014, **https://socialinnovation.blog.jbs.cam.ac.uk/2014/10/20/public-sector-intraprenurship-overcoming-bureaucratic-immune-systems/**.

In corporate terms, a start-up is a bit like a virus. There are lots of them, and there aren't a lot of resources invested in any one of them. Most of them will fail, like most mutations of a virus. And that's okay, because some of them will succeed spectacularly. Viruses don't need immune systems and start-ups don't need bureaucracy. On the other hand, a huge corporation or global public accounting firm[192] has hundreds of thousands of employees, a long history, and a lot to lose. They're more like humans or other complex organisms, where uncontrolled mutation is likely to be harmful because it introduces a disruptive change with unforeseeable, unfortunate consequences. If every self-assured extremist in a big organization had their own way, the place would fall apart pretty quickly in a storm of chaos.

Of course, to extend the analogy, sometimes the immune system misfires. You get overreactions like allergies or autoimmune diseases. The risk in large organizations is that the bureaucracy has turned into the organizational equivalent of lupus or ulcerative colitis. It has become too stubborn, and is impairing the effective function of the body.

If the individual stubbornness of extremism leads to chaos, the organizational stubbornness of bureaucracy leads to stagnation. I once tried to have a boilerplate clause removed from one of our standard letters. The clause wasn't harmful, but it was confusing and clients often pushed back on it. Everyone involved decided it was more trouble than it was worth, and should be eliminated. Except... no one knew who had inserted it in the letter in the first place. It could have come from any of four different risk management functions within the firm, but no one in any of those functions remembered having asked for it. You'd think that would make it easy to remove. You'd be wrong. Because no one knew who had put it in, no one was willing to take responsibility for taking it out. It took me years, and being in charge of three of the four functions, to finally get it eliminated.[193]

---

[192] Technically there's no such thing as a "global public accounting firm" – the largest firms are networks of autonomous local partnerships.

[193] In a supreme irony, a regulatory change taking effect in 2025 (PCAOB Rule EI 1000.03.c(1)) requires it to be put back in.

An ossified bureaucracy may not just impose unnecessary burdens. Like a defective immune system, its inefficient function may miss the very threats it's intended to prevent. When I was working on updating our engagement acceptance system, we found that in some cases it could require half a dozen or more partners to sign off. Those sign-offs were each put in place to address a threat of some sort. And in theory, they should have collectively reduced risk. The problem is that if six people are signing off on something, the first one might very well say, "I know five more people are going to look at this, so I don't need to look at it very closely." And the sixth person might say, "I know five people already looked at this, so I don't need to look at it very closely." Jason Brennan cites the example of B.F. Goodrich delivering faulty brake assemblies to the U.S. Air Force in the 1960s. Each person in the chain of sign-offs, many of whom knew the brakes were defective, decided that raising the issue was someone else's problem. As Brennan notes:

> *When people see a problem and think they're the only ones who can help, they do. When they see a problem but lots of people could help, they don't – or at least they are far less likely to do so.*[194]

There is abundant experimental psychological research to that effect, which is why in CPR classes we are taught to instruct one specific bystander to call 911, not simply shout, "Someone call 911!" So not only can bureaucracy induce paralysis; the well-meaning diffusion of responsibility across multiple people, intended to mitigate risk, actually increases the risk it was supposed to reduce.

And yet, the stubbornness of the bureaucracy is no less based on sincere belief than the stubbornness of extremists. The belief is just different. As David Brooks puts it:

---

[194] Brennan, English, Hasnas, and Jaworski, *Business Ethics for Better Behavior*, "Why Aren't We All Saints."

Organizations are trying to protect themselves from lawsuits, but the whole administrative apparatus comes with an implied view of human nature. People are weak, fragile, vulnerable and kind of stupid. They need administrators to run their lives. They have to be trained never to take initiative, lest they wander off into activities that are deemed by the authorities to be out of bounds.[195]

Fiction authors have toyed with the notion of law versus chaos for decades. The theme of those opposing forces runs through Michael Moorcock's fantasy works and the science fiction universe of Babylon Five. The conclusion is always that either one, out of balance, is sterile. Worse, they're both oppressive. Neither extremism nor bureaucracy tolerates dissent or listens to the arguments of others, just as Pharaoh didn't listen to Moses in the face of overwhelming evidence. Pharaoh, of course, squared the circle of stubbornness by embodying the overwhelming bureaucracy of a powerful state in the person of one individual.

~~~

One of the best indictments of stubbornness is the quote, usually misattributed to Albert Einstein, that "insanity is doing the same thing over and over again and expecting different results."[196] By that definition, many of us are insane much of the time, because we won't break out of established patterns of thought, even if they're counterproductive. As we've seen above, that goes for individuals as well as organizations. While it's not possible or useful to continually reexamine every single belief, decision, and opinion, we stick to them past the point where it's beneficial. Cialdini summarizes the dilemma:

---

[195] Brooks, David, "Death by a Thousand Paper Cuts," *The New York Times,* January 18, 2024.
[196] Quote Investigator (**https://quoteinvestigator.com/2017/03/23/same/**) sources this statement most reliably to 1981, from an (appropriately) anonymous member of Alcoholics Anonymous. Alice Alaprice in *The Ultimate Quotable Einstein* (2010) states that there is no evidence that Einstein ever made the statement.

*But since automatic consistency is so useful in allowing us
an economical and appropriate way of behaving most of the
time, we can't decide merely to eliminate it from our lives
altogether. The results would be disastrous.... The only way
out of the dilemma is to know when such consistency is likely
to lead to a poor choice.*[197]

That's easier said than done. We're usually stubborn about strongly held
beliefs which are, by definition, strongly held. We are unlikely to challenge
them easily, and to some extent rightly so. Established tradition and culture
can be critical antidotes not just to aimless dithering, but also to catastrophic
experimentation. As Alan Bloom said of the consequences of Nietzsche's
radical openness to all forms of morality beyond good and evil, "when one
ventures out into the vast open spaces opened up by Nietzsche, it is hard to
set limits."[198]

Here are some approaches that may help identify and address the problem of
when individual and organizational consistency have reached the point of
counterproductive stubbornness:

(1) Approach every issue with intellectual humility;

(2) Encourage respectful dissent;

(3) Take a fact-based approach to problem solving; and

(4) Understand that the ends generally don't justify the means.

I had the privilege in college of taking a class from Dr. David Linowes, an
advisor to four U.S. presidents and the father of socioeconomic
accounting.[199] He was a pioneer in the field of corporate social
responsibility, and he put up with a lot more of my crap than I deserved as an
undergraduate. I would routinely quote Milton Friedman at him and he had a
great deal of patience for me, despite the fact that he surely understood
Friedman a hundred times better than I did.

---

[197] Cialdini, *Influence*, "Commitment and Consistency."
[198] Bloom, *The Closing of the American Mind*, "Values."
[199] Lynn, Andrea, "Former U. of I. political economist, adviser to four U.S. presidents, dies at
90," *University of Illinois Urbana-Champaign News Bureau*, November 1, 2007,
https://news.illinois.edu/view/6367/206486.

Linowes was very fond of two-by-two matrices. One of them had "intelligence" on one axis and "ambition" on the other. He said that everyone in the class must be smart and ambitious, because otherwise we wouldn't be taking an elective class on corporate social responsibility. He also said that people in the "smart and ambitious" quadrant were dangerous.

It seems fair to assume that you're smart and ambitious or you wouldn't be reading this book. I certainly think I'm pretty smart. I graduated summa cum laude, highest honors, phi beta kappa, bronze tablet, you name it. I was the partner in charge of multiple functions in one of the world's largest professional services firms. And the question you're asking right now is, "Good for you, so what?"

That is exactly the right question. I made some fabulously bad predictions all within the course of about a year in the early 1990s, specifically that Apple would go bankrupt, Fidel Castro wouldn't last a year after the fall of the Soviet Union, and no one would ever want to use the world wide web for anything. I spent most of my career working in a field – financial due diligence – where my mistakes became fairly obvious fairly quickly. And I made mistakes. You can be smart and still be wrong – a lot.

I also had the privilege of spending a lot of time around people smarter than me. Some of my high school classmates include the dean of the physics department at Stanford, a winner of multiple technical Academy Awards, a Nebula Award winning science fiction author, and so forth. All smarter than me. And I know that all of them were also wrong – a lot.

Ibn Khaldun summarizes the limits of individual knowledge perfectly: "Admission of one's ignorance is a specific religious duty."[200]

We need to embrace the humility that comes from realizing that we are not gods, or omniscient beings. Many of our beliefs, even some that are strongly held, are going to be mistaken. That's why we need to embrace discussion and dissent, as Edmund Burke notes:

---

[200] Ibn Khaldun, *The Muqqadimah*, Introduction.

I have known and, according to my measure, have co-operated with great men; and I have never yet seen any plan which has not been mended by the observation of those who were much inferior in understanding to the person who took the lead in the business.[201]

There are many different approaches as a leader to achieving "high performing teams," but in my organizations we used Patrick Lencioni's model.[202] It takes a pyramid approach, where each step on the pyramid is foundational to those above. Many teams try to jump straight to commitment and accountability, which are the third and fourth layers, while passing over trust and constructive conflict, which are the first and second layers. It makes sense to me that you can't get team members to commit to a plan if they haven't had the opportunity to debate it. Of course, debate has two purposes – to obtain buy-in, but more importantly to leverage the perspective of the team to come up with a better plan, as Burke recommends above. Ideally the combination of trust and constructive conflict creates the psychological safety that Haidt mentioned as the key indicator of a healthy work environment.[203]

Many of my successes weren't really mine, and many of the failures I avoided were through the intervention of others. In my intranet site example in Chapter Three, I would have implemented an inferior version without the intervention of my team. Earlier in this chapter I mentioned that I nearly rejected a compliance intervention as burdensome, annoying, and probably unhelpful. In fact, I would have rejected it if others hadn't pushed me to do it, and it was the only thing that actually worked.

Humbly navigating stubbornness requires not just dissent, discussion, and debate, but also data. In the absence of data, the discussion is just argument. At some point, one of Pharaoh's advisors should have said, "You know, this God character has already hit us with plagues of frogs, gnats, flies, locusts… the evidence is that he's more powerful than we are. Maybe we should quit while we're ahead."

---

[201] Burke, *Reflections on the Revolution in France.*
[202] Lencioni, Patrick, *The Five Dysfunctions of a Team* (Jossey-Bass, 2011).
[203] Haidt, *The Anxious Generation*, "Discover Mode and the Need for Risky Play."

I would have been thrilled to drop the burdensome and annoying compliance intervention if it hadn't worked. So would everyone else. But we had A/B testing to show its effectiveness. One population received every other intervention except that one. The other population received them all. The population that received every intervention got dramatically better, while the one that received all the others actually got worse. When we introduced the final intervention to the first population, it improved dramatically as well. It made little sense to me that the intervention worked as well as it did, but the evidence was incredibly strong.

In any undertaking involving human behavior, the results are rarely what we expect. I could have added "unpredictable" to the list of human characteristics. Technology companies are relentlessly data driven. They A/B test every option, taking whatever works best, regardless of which option seemed like it "should" be better.[204] As Thomas Sowell put it:

> *In the constrained vision, any individual's own knowledge alone is grossly inadequate for social decision-making, and often even for his own personal decisions…. Knowledge as conceived in the constrained vision is predominantly experience… winnowing out in Darwinian competition what works from what does not work.*[205]

While being data-driven may seem like a modern idea, Alexander Hamilton had much the same view two centuries before Sowell. Citing David Hume, he notes:

---

[204] An idea credited to Chamath Palihapitiya of Facebook in Jeff Orlowski's *The Social Dilemma* (Netflix, 2020). I've been told anecdotally that Chinese technology companies are even more ruthless about A/B testing than U.S. technology companies.
[205] Thomas Sowell, *A Conflict of Visions*, (Basic Books, 2007), original text 1987, "The Mobilization of Knowledge."

To balance a large state or society (says he), whether monarchical or republican, on general laws, is a work of so great difficulty, that no human genius, however comprehensive, is able, by the mere dint of reason and reflection, to effect it. The judgments of many must unite in the work; experience must guide the labor; time must bring it to perfection, and the feeling of inconveniences must correct the mistakes which they inevitably fall into in their first trials and experiments.[206]

Finally, being humble and data driven implies that the ends generally don't justify the means. Why? Because we can have only limited confidence in what ends we're actually going to achieve with a particular set of means. As Edmund Burke put it, "The means taught by experience may be better suited to political ends than those contrived in the original project." [207]

Alinksy strenuously disagreed with that notion, dismissing the idea as cowardly. But as much as I admire quite a bit of Alinksy's thought, I believe he's wrong here. I've seen too many coups go wrong, in both the political and business world, where deposing one unacceptable leader created a situation that was even worse. The Second Gulf War stands out as a clear example of an intervention not going as planned, where the lives lost in the formal combat phase paled by comparison to the lives lost in the insurgency that followed. Similarly, I've seen companies where a conspiracy to bring down a leader led to a replacement even less acceptable to the conspirators.

Alinsky is understandably concerned that moral dithering can stand in the way of getting anything done. He says:

---

[206] Hamilton, Alexander, *The Federalist Papers*, Federalist 85, 1788. I've been unable to find the original in Hume's writings.
[207] Burke, *Reflections on the Revolution in France.*

> *In action, one does not always enjoy the luxury of a decision*
> *that is consistent both with one's individual conscience and*
> *the good of mankind. The choice must be for the latter....*
> *Means and ends are so qualitatively interrelated that the*
> *true question has never been the proverbial one, "Does the*
> *End justify the Means?" but always has been "Does this*
> *particular end justify this particular means?"[208]*

That may hold true when we have very high confidence that our means will achieve our desired ends – which is frequently inconsistent with the premises of humility, dissent, and data-driven decision-making. And even when we do know the ends with certainty, I'm still not sure Alinsky is right due to second- and third-order consequences. Alinsky writes that, "Geneva rules on treatment of prisoners or use of nuclear weapons are observed only because the enemy or his potential allies may retaliate."[209] But that's not the only reason. When fighting against terrorists, we don't treat enemy combatants humanely because we believe they will treat our soldiers humanely in turn – we know they won't. We treat enemy combatants humanely because we don't want to turn our soldiers into the kind of people who treat others inhumanely. The cost of war is high enough without inflicting that psychic damage on our servicemen and women.

Sowell here takes a view almost directly opposite Alinsky, in which he recognizes human inability to achieve what he calls "cosmic justice" and recommends instead the more limited "formal" justice:

> *Cosmic justice is not about the rules of the game. It is about*
> *putting particular segments of society in the position that*
> *they would have been in but for some undeserved misfortune.*
> *This conception of fairness requires that third parties must*
> *wield the power to control outcomes, over-riding rules,*
> *standards, or the preferences of other people.*

---

[208] Alinsky, *Rules for Radicals*, "Of Means and Ends."
[209] Ibid.

The challenge of determining the net balance of numerous windfall advantages and disadvantages for one individual at one given time is sufficiently daunting. To attempt the same for whole broad-brush categories of people, each in differing stages of their individual life cycles, in a complex and changing society, suggests hubris.[210]

Once that hubris kicks in and we decide that the ends justify the means, we start down the path of Sam Bankman-Fried's corrupted version of "effective altruism" where any means of making money, including stealing from your customers, is justifiable as long as the theoretical uses for the money are noble. The better approach, it seems to me, is the intellectual honesty advocated by Holman Jenkins: "We tell the truth and let the chips fall because *we don't know* where the chips will finally land even if we think we do."[211]

Overcoming pathological stubbornness requires balance. Too much deference to the "rules of the game" can result in paralyzing bureaucracy. Too greatly prizing our own view of what's best can lead to pig-headed extremism. And of course, questioning every single decision can lead to unproductive dithering, or gutless blowing in the wind of others' opinions. The right approach blends humility, discussion, and analytical rigor.

[210] Sowell, Thomas, *The Quest for Cosmic Justice,* (The Free Press, 1999), Ch.1.
[211] Jenkins, Holman, "Trump's Best Lies Weren't Trump's," *The Wall Street Journal*, May 7, 2024.

V. Ungrateful

"What have you done for me lately?"

\-   Janet Jackson

God didn't just use the plagues to deliver the Israelites from slavery in Egypt. He also parted the Red Sea so they could pass through on dry land, and then closed it again to drown Pharaoh's pursuing army. Exodus 15:1-21 is the Israelites' song of praise to the Lord.

Three sentences later at Exodus 15:24, "the people grumbled against Moses, saying, 'What are we to drink?'"

Six sentences after that, the Israelites are on the verge of open rebellion, protesting:

> *"If only we had died at the Lord's hand in the land of Egypt,*
> *as we sat by our kettles of meat and ate our fill of bread!*
> *But you have led us into this wilderness to make this whole*
> *assembly die of famine!"*[212]

God proceeded to give the Israelites manna from heaven, and water springing forth from rock. Then he gave them the Ten Commandments to establish an eternal covenant with his chosen people. And literally while Moses was up on the mountain receiving God's law, the Israelites built a golden calf as a new god to worship:

> *"Come, make us a god who will go before us; as for that*
> *man Moses who brought us out of Egypt, we do not know*
> *what has happened to him."*[213]

---

[212] Exodus 16:3.
[213] Exodus 32:1. It's not entirely clear whether the golden calf was supposed to represent God (whom the Israelites had been forbidden to visibly represent) or some other god. What is clear is the Israelites' lack of faith and gratitude after a series of miracles.

Ingratitude is so obvious that social psychologists like Haidt and Wright don't even bother to explain it. It's intuitively obvious that betraying someone once they're no longer useful to you is a strategy for success. Haidt and Wright focus instead on why people are occasionally grateful. Haidt credits "loyalty" as one of the six moral foundations,[214] while Wright discusses the evolutionary basis for why it might arise, specifically the notion of reciprocal altruism.[215] Reciprocal altruism means what it sounds like. If you're nice to me, I'll be nice to you. If you're mean to me, I'll be mean to you. Wright documents the evolutionary advantages of reciprocal altruism, which looks a lot like gratitude.

The problem is, humans know we can reap the social benefits of gratitude without actually being grateful. As Wright notes:

> *But when it doesn't – when we can look nice without really being so nice, or can be profitably mean without getting caught – don't be surprised if an ugly part of human nature surfaces. Hence secret betrayals of all gradations, from the everyday to the Shakespearean.*[216]

What's interesting is that the betrayals don't even have to be secret. Humans stab other humans in the back, but if we think we can get away with it, we'll stab them in the front too. The Israelites grumbled so much directly to the prophet who led them out of Egypt that he was afraid they'd stone him to death, and then they set up the golden calf right at the foot of the mountain where God's most spectacular theophany was taking place. And maybe that's the darkest side of reciprocal altruism – it only works as long as we think we can continue to get something out of the other person. Moses had led the Israelites out of slavery in Egypt, but "what had he done for them lately?"

---

[214] Haidt, *The Righteous Mind*, "The Moral Foundations of Politics."
[215] Wright, *The Moral Animal*, "Friends."
[216] Ibid.

We all like to believe we're like Hachiko, the noble dog who waited nine years at the train station for his master to return.[217] But we're probably more like cats, which will eat their owners the moment they stop breathing.[218] That most famously cynical of men, Nicolo Machiavelli, said:

> *Because this is to be asserted in general of men, that they are ungrateful, fickle, false, cowardly, covetous, and as long as you succeed they are yours entirely; they will offer you their blood, property, life, and children, as is said above, when the need is far distant; but when it approaches they turn against you.[219]*

Because we're selfish and jealous, we're quick to take credit for our success and blame others for our failures. That lets us easily rationalize betrayal of those others by saying we're simply getting what we deserve, what we've earned by our own merits. What may have been the most widely remembered line from the 2012 U.S. presidential election was President Obama's statement that "If you've got a business, you didn't build that."

Not only the Romney campaign but many pundits and journalists pounced on that line, arguing that it showed Obama's leftist tendency to discredit private enterprise and exalt the state. To be honest, the statement irritated me too, even though in context it seems entirely reasonable:

---

[217] "A Tale of Unbound Loyalty: Hachiko, the Dog who Waited for 9 Years for his Master's Return," *Unbelievable Facts,* 2013, **https://unbelievable-facts.com/2013/05/the-tale-unbound-loyalty-hachiko.html.**

[218] I exaggerate for effect, and studies appear to be lacking, but there does seem to be some evidence that cats are likelier than dogs to eat their dead owners, see for example, Coren, Stanley, "If You Died Alone, Would Your Cat or Dog Eat You," *Psychology Today*, February 8, 2024.

[219] Machiavelli, Nicolo, *The Prince*, trans. W.K. Marriott (Wisehouse, 2015), original text 1532, Ch.XVII. I have to get in a Machiavelli quote. When I took a social psychology class as an undergraduate decades ago, we were given the MACH-IV test of Machiavellianism and asked to self-report our scores. Mine was the highest. To which I responded that anyone who had scored higher than I did would lie about it. And yes, you're remembering correctly that I believe I have mild autism spectrum disorder, which makes for a strange combination with Machiavellianism. I'm a strange person.

*If you were successful, somebody along the line gave you
some help. There was a great teacher somewhere in your
life. Somebody helped to create this unbelievable American
system that we have that allowed you to thrive. Somebody
invested in roads and bridges. If you've got a business, you
didn't build that. Somebody else made that happen.*[220]

There's no way to get inside President Obama's head to know exactly what
he meant by the word "that" in the last two sentences, but it seems fair to
assume he was referring to the roads, and the bridges, and the overall system.
A modern economy is an incredibly complex and interrelated undertaking. I
can't think of a responsible economist who would assert that one hundred
percent of any success comes solely from one individual's genius and effort.
But Obama's speech produced a massive backlash. Some of that may have
been due to people taking the quote out of context. I also think that for a
speaker of his talent, it was unusually artlessly phrased. But I believe some
of the controversy was also due to the fact that the speech challenged people
to be more grateful, which we don't like to be.

In Western societies and the U.S. in particular we practically fetishize
independence, and for fairly obvious reasons. As Steven Pinker says, "Social
animals risk theft, cannibalism, cuckoldry, infanticide, extortion, and other
treachery." Since it isn't feasible to opt out of the society of others entirely,
"They exchange favors, repay and enforce debts, punish cheaters, and join
coalitions."[221] Which is fine, except that we also welch on our debts and
betray our coalition partners when they're no longer useful to us.

Biblically speaking, salvation history has brought us full circle. Humanity's
fall began with our selfishness in Genesis, when Adam and Eve weren't
satisfied with the paradise God created and wanted to be gods themselves.
After all the work of the patriarchs, Moses, and God himself to rebuild the
broken covenant, the Israelites (who stand in for all of us) reject it again
through their ingratitude.

---

[220] Obama, Barack, Campaign speech in Roanoke VA, July 23, 2012,
https://www.factcheck.org/2012/07/you-didnt-build-that-uncut-and-unedited/.
[221] Pinker, *How the Mind Works,* "Revenge of the Nerds."

At the risk of sounding like the cranky old man that I am, I suggest that we see those effects to this day in our throwaway culture, where every relationship from romance to employment is treated as temporary and disposable. In fact, we might be getting worse.

While the divorce rate in the U.S. has fallen since its peak in the 1980s, my reading of the data is that it's only because fewer couples are getting married at all. According to the Institute for Family Studies, the U.S. marriage rate hit an all-time low in 2019.[222] Among "ever-married" women, the number who are currently divorced is higher now than ever, having risen from less than 1% in 1900 to over 20% in 2018.[223]

Human relationships seem to be moving from a concept of "Until death do us part" to "Until I find something better."

Was some amount of historical commitment to relationships biologically mediated? Yes, almost certainly. Before birth control, if you had sex, there was a pretty good chance of pregnancy, and then you were likely stuck in a marriage whether you liked it or not. Limited economic opportunities for women meant they couldn't leave, and if men didn't like being stuck with their wife, they tended to cheat and to a large extent get away with it. As numerous priests have pointed out in homilies I've heard, what happened to the guy who was with the woman caught in adultery? No one was talking about stoning him to death.[224]

In that sense, more freedom in relationships is almost certainly a good thing. Not many people in the West would advocate for arranged marriages, for example. But have we perhaps gone a little too far in treating relationship partners as commodities? Freya India writes:

---

[222] Wang, Wendy, "The U.S. Divorce Rate Has Hit a 50-Year Low," *Institute for Family Studies*, November 10, 2020, **https://ifstudies.org/blog/the-us-divorce-rate-has-hit-a-50-year-low**.
[223] Schweizer, Valerie, "Divorce: More than a Century of Change, 1900-2018," *Bowling Green State University National Center for Family & Marriage Research*, 2020, **https://www.bgsu.edu/ncfmr/resources/data/family-profiles/schweizer-divorce-century-change-1900-2018-fp-20-22.html**.
[224] John 8:3-5.

*We talk about how bad being ghosted is for our mental
health, and how being swiped past destroys our self-esteem.
But don't they also just make us **horrible**? Funny how we
never talk about **who we become** when we use these apps;
how we behave. Honestly I feel more pity for those
relentlessly swiping and ghosting people than the ones who
keep getting rejected. Isn't that the real tragedy? It's
terrible to be treated like some disposable product but
worse, I think, to watch yourself shopping for another
person, to know you're judging them on the most superficial
standards that you would hate someone to judge you on, to
act in this psychopathic way when you're paying premium to
access "**Your** Top Picks" of **human beings**.* [225]

To be fair to modern culture, to some extent we've always "shopped for
another person" – read Jane Austen's *Pride and Prejudice* for a description
of how it worked in pre-Victorian England. And the process has long been
somewhat commercial, whether that meant paying the village matchmaker or
shelling out college tuition in the hopes of obtaining an "Mrs" degree. [226]
Human relationships have always been somewhat transactional. The internet
makes the transactions quicker and more obvious. While that may improve
transparency, that's not necessarily a good thing. A purely transactional
relationship creates no gratitude. There's no reciprocal altruism, only
reciprocity. "I do X for you, you do Y for me, we go our separate ways."
It's not pretty, but it's human.

Indeed, the ingratitude problem has been part of human relationships since
the ancient world. Jesus explained that "Because of the hardness of your
hearts Moses allowed you to divorce your wives." [227] I take that to means that
without a mechanism for divorce, the ancient Israelites would have simply
abandoned their wives or maybe even killed them once they decided to trade
up to a newer model.

---

[225] India, Freya and Jonathan Haidt, "On the Degrading Effects of Life Online, Part 2," *After Babel*, May 14, 2024, **https://www.afterbabel.com/p/degrading-effects-of-life-online**.
[226] While I didn't know anyone in college who was seeking an "Mrs" degree, my wife had friends in her chemical engineering program in Chile who were definitely doing so – which seems like a lot of effort considering how difficult the chemical engineering program was.
[227] Matthew 19:8.

~~~

If transactional relationships are a problem in romance, are they a problem in employment? In the United States, employment is generally "at will."[228] Either party can terminate the employment relationship whenever they want, with an appropriate (usually short) notice period. There are exceptions such as tenured professors and those represented by public or private sector unions, but most of us are employed "at will."

That carries a lot of benefits. On the employee side, being allowed to leave the job whenever you want prevents indentured servitude, slavery, and human trafficking. On the employer side, employment at will facilitates the "creative destruction"[229] of the market economy. The company is free to improve margins through automation, outsourcing, offshoring, or whatever else may increase efficiency. There's a reason why U.S. companies tend to be more efficient than European companies, whose labor laws are more restrictive.

The problem is that if employment is purely transactional, if it's all about "what have you done for me lately," there can be no gratitude or loyalty. We feed a dark side of the human psyche.

My biggest contribution to public accounting was probably made 25 years ago, when I co-authored the "S[tuff] rolls downhill" PowerPoint. A colleague (Greg Moskoff) and I sketched it on a whiteboard at our audit client late one night, and I turned it into a very rudimentary PowerPoint presentation.[230] Another colleague forwarded it to "a couple of friends." We were horrified when, a week later, we started getting it forwarded to us from people at other public accounting firms. Since then, I've seen it repurposed for engineering companies, investment banks, advertising agencies, and a particularly slick animated version for the U.S. Air Force.[231] For a while it was informally included in training in public accounting firms.

---

[228] "At-will employment," Wikimedia Foundation, last modified January 26, 2025, **https://en.wikipedia.org/wiki/At-will_employment**.

[229] Schumpeter, Joseph, *Capitalism, Socialism and Democracy*, (LeBooks) original text 1942, "The Process of Creative Destruction."

[230] I'm pretty sure this version is a faithful reproduction of the original, which I no longer have: **https://www.reddit.com/r/consulting/comments/9x462a/the_crest_of_ignorance/**.

[231]

https://www.reddit.com/r/AirForce/comments/27drp6/how_crap_rolls_downhill_in_the_air_force/.

I'm convinced the unique genius of the presentation was the "crest of ignorance" in the shape of the hill, which Greg invented. The crest of ignorance keeps the s[tuff] from rolling down to the lowest level and instead keeps a mid-level professional (in the original version, the audit senior) submerged in it. There is also a "cave of unreported exceptions" at the bottom where the lowest level staff can shovel in more s[tuff], which begins to ferment and bubbles up to the mid-level professionals, further adding to their misery.

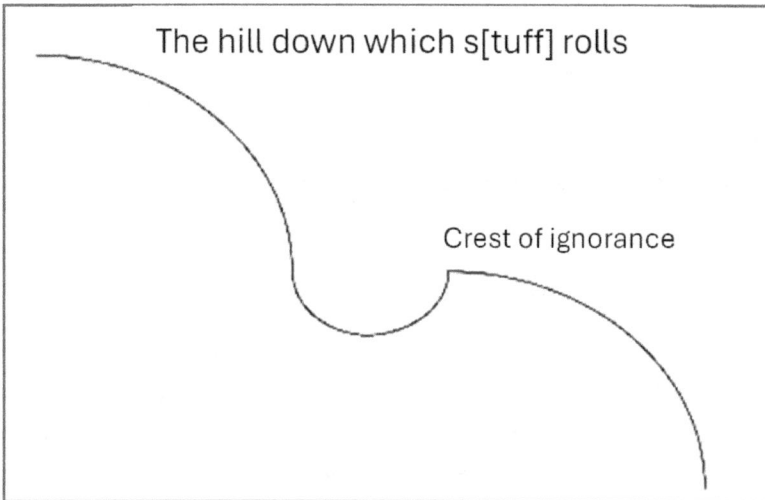

The hill down which s[tuff] rolls

Crest of ignorance

The reason I think it resonates so much is that everyone, at pretty much every level, can identify with taking s[tuff] from those above, while not being able to fully pass it on to those below. We all ask, "Why am I the only one who has to put up with all this s[tuff]?"

How does that relate to ingratitude? Because we all inherently view our success as due to our own merits, but every setback as caused by someone else, whether it's our overbearing superiors or our incompetent subordinates. Thus the negative reaction to Obama's "you didn't build that" comment. To some extent we all tend to think, "Not only did I build that without any help, the rest of you just made it harder."

If we can internalize success and externalize failure, we don't have to be grateful. "Sure, God may have hit the Egyptians with some plagues, but now he's stuck us out in the desert and our prophet has vanished up a mountain. What's up with that?" If we don't have to be grateful, then we're freed from the obligations of reciprocal altruism, and can go back to being fully selfish.

Ingratitude is only a half step removed from betrayal. If you feel that you don't owe someone anything, you can do whatever you want with them. It doesn't matter how long they've been with you, or what they've done for you.

Dante consigns betrayers to the ninth circle of hell.[232]

That's all well and good biblically, but does it matter in practice for an organization? Given the efficiency benefits of at will employment, don't those outweigh any vague feelings of discomfort about disloyalty or ingratitude?

Not according to Ibn Khaldun. He emphasizes the need for "asabiyyah" to control a group.[233] My translation of the Muqaddimah renders the term as "group feeling," but I've also seen it translated as "social cohesion" or "solidarity." Ibn Khaldun associates solidarity with a tribe or lineage, but the principle applies broadly to any group endeavor. Indeed, the Solidarity trade union in Poland successfully resisted the totalitarian government, "widely recognized as having played a central role in the end of communist rule in Poland."[234]

Japan provides an example of organizations that strive to create long-lasting employment relationships. Japan's "lifetime employment" concept is not literally that.

> *Lifetime employment is a long-established practice in large*
> *Japanese firms. However, it is a "gentlemen's agreement"*
> *and is not guaranteed by statute or collective bargaining*
> *agreement.*[235]

---

[232] Alighieri, *The Divine Comedy*, "Inferno."

[233] Ibn Khaldun, *The Muqaddimah*, Introduction.

[234] "Solidarity (Polish trade union)," Wikimedia Foundation, last modified January 9, 2025, **https://en.wikipedia.org/wiki/Solidarity_(Polish_trade_union)**.

[235] Kazutoshi, Koshiro, "Lifetime employment in Japan: three models of the concept," *Bureau of Labor Statistics*, 1984, **https://www.bls.gov/opub/mlr/1984/08/rpt4full.pdf**.

However, there is certainly a deliberate focus on long-term employee retention, with the intention of building skills and creating a shared sense of mission and culture.

> *By taking a long-term view of human resource development, Japanese companies aim at fostering a sense of organisational unity as well as the efficient formation and accumulation of business-specific skills.*[236]

There are definitely benefits to the greater flexibility of the U.S.'s "at-will" approach. We also need to be careful of "in-group" dynamics, which can start to resemble nepotism or produce discrimination. The problem with creating a loyal, favored "in-group" is that it necessarily creates a disfavored "out-group" that is discriminated against, even if only unconsciously. A salient example is legacy college admissions. While there might seem to be good reasons of loyalty to give preference to the children of alumni and faculty, it can reach extremes. For example, at Harvard, "recruited athletes, legacies, relatives of donors and children of faculty and staff... make up less than 5 percent of applicants, but around 30 percent of those admitted each year."[237] That clearly suggests that a valuable resource (admission to Harvard) is being withheld from others who may be more deserving. And it isn't just in the Ivy League – something similar happened at my alma mater, the University of Illinois.[238] Patterns of loyalty can harden into entrenched group privilege.[239]

---

[236] OECD, "Creating Responsive Adult Learning Opportunities in Japan," February 22, 2021, https://www.oecd.org/en/publications/creating-responsive-adult-learning-opportunities-in-japan_cfe1ccd2-en.html.

[237] Shear, Michael and Anemona Hartocollis, "Education Dept. Opens Civil Rights Inquiry into Harvard's Legacy Admissions," *The New York Times*, July 25, 2023.

[238] Cohen, Jodi, Stacy St. Clair and Tara Malone, "Clout Goes to College," *The Chicago Tribune*, May 29, 2009.

[239] Contributing to scholarships and outreach to underrepresented populations can help mitigate that problem. For example, the REACH enrichment program at Regis High School in New York City (https://www.regis.org/reach/) "empowers high-achieving young men from underserved communities as Catholic leaders committed to faith, scholarship, and service." The U of I's Illinois Promise Fund is intended to "ensure the affordability of higher education for students from the lowest income levels," usually first generation college students (https://osfa.illinois.edu/types-of-aid/other-aid/illinois-promise/).

However, my experience suggest that on balance, loyalty and retention are important and positive in most organizational settings. In my years analyzing the telecom industry, one of the key metrics was churn. Churn simply means how many existing customers you lose, and is shown as a percentage of the customers leaving the network in the period divided by the total number of customers.[240] The same metric is used by human resources organizations for employees.

In telecom, churn is unequivocally bad because it costs money to acquire a new subscriber through advertising, discounted hardware, and so forth. And a new customer is likely to be less loyal than an old one, and is thus more likely to churn again if a competitor offers better rates.

Similar issues apply in human resources. It costs money to recruit a new employee, and then unproductive time to get them up to speed. And the new recruit is, all else equal, more likely than a twenty-year veteran to leave again for a better opportunity elsewhere.

Over my time in public accounting, churn increased dramatically. I have heard statistics cited that these days the average tenure of public accounting personnel (including partners) is around two years. For example, CPA Practice Advisor notes "many firms experiencing an average turnover rate of up to 25 percent per year" and goes on to observe that:

> *A study conducted by Cornell University estimated that the average cost per turnover ranges from 30 percent of the annual salary for that position when the employee is paid hourly. Expenses associated with turnover include the cost of advertising open positions, paying someone to train new hires, and lost productivity as new hires are on-boarded.*[241]

---

[240] Like most metrics in the telecom sector, it's a little more complex in terms of exactly what goes into the numerator and the denominator, and isn't always measured consistently.

[241] CPA Practice Advisor, "How CPA Firms Can Reduce Staff Turnover and Boost Profits," May 27, 2015, **https://www.cpapracticeadvisor.com/2015/05/27/how-cpa-firms-can-reduce-staff-turnover-and-boost-profits/18872/**.

The turnover rate seems to be increasing. When I taught a "quality for engagement leaders" course, I would start by asking how many participants (who ranged from senior managers to partners) were lifers at the firm or another Big Four public accounting firm. When I began teaching the course in 2012, around 80% were lifetime Big Four veterans, with 20% coming from industry or other consultancies. By 2020 when I stopped teaching the course, the ratio had roughly flipped to 20% veterans, 80% people who were new to public accounting.

The economic cost of employee churn is clear from the CPA Advisor article. I believe there's also a significant intangible cost.

A key benefit of having a mission is to get from "I" to "we" – channeling human selfishness from something focused purely on the mundane (getting ahead) to the sacred (a larger, cooperative, awe-inspiring goal). Going from "chimp-ish" to "bee-ish" in Haidt's formulation. But there's probably nothing quite so effective at reducing cooperative, "bee-ish" behavior as knowing that your organization feels no loyalty to you. And as a result, you feel no loyalty to it. Bees will sting a threat to the hive even though it kills them, because they have the ultimate group feeling. In that case, Ibn Khaldun's idea of group feeling arising from lineage is exactly right – all the bees in a hive are siblings.

For humans to sacrifice themselves for others is harder. Successful militaries are the best example. They get people to do extremely counterintuitive things like running towards gunfire, not away from it, by building group feeling. That involves not just extensive training to build a sense of unity, but also concepts like "no one left behind" that date back at least to the Greeks and Romans (the term is "nemo resideo" in Latin). Modern armies focus on loyalty, not pay.[242] The historical use of unattached soldiers for hire led to the following observation by Machiavelli:

---

[242] Notwithstanding reports that contractors outnumbered U.S. troops in recent conflicts, those contractors generally served in logistics, maintenance, and translation roles, not combat operations – see for example Leo Shane's "Report: Contractors outnumber U.S. troops in Afghanistan 3-to-1" in *The Military Times*, August 17, 2016.

Mercenaries and auxiliaries are useless and dangerous; and if one holds his state based on these arms, he will stand neither firm nor safe; for they are disunited, ambitious, and without discipline, unfaithful, valiant before friends, cowardly before enemies.[243]

People who are in it just for the money will turn on you when they think it's to their advantage. Vladimir Putin's use of the Wagner Group demonstrated Machiavelli's insight when the mercenary army launched an ill-fated coup against him. In a crunch, when you need someone to have your back, loyalty is a better currency than cash.

Companies conducting massive layoffs to maintain profitability is almost the opposite of "no one left behind." Layoffs can certainly help economics in the short-term. As the joke goes, "People really must be our most valuable asset – every time we fire a bunch of them, our stock price goes up."[244] But it undermines trust and group cohesion. I was saved from a round of layoffs during the financial crisis by allies who moved me into risk management. I was able to return the favor by moving people into my group who were being laid off from client service. Those individuals were valuable contributors with solid performance reviews, who were just in the wrong place at the wrong time.

There are of course reasons why employees might need to be let go. Maybe they're dishonest, or lazy, or incompetent, or their job has become obsolete and they can't be retrained. Maybe the business can truly only survive through cost cutting. But many times competent, productive employees are terminated for short-term profitability, even knowing that they will likely need to be replaced later at a higher cost. I don't intend to analyze the economics of those decisions. Rather, I suggest that there is a corrosive effect on culture.

---

[243] Machiavelli, *The Prince*, Ch.XII.
[244] I can't find the source for that joke. It sounds like something from Scott Adams' Dilbert, which might explain why it's vanished from the internet.

When the employment relationship is short-term and transactional, everyone throughout the hierarchy is always asking, "What have you done for me lately?" If I believe my employer is loyal to me, I will be inclined to stay even if another opportunity is available elsewhere at a higher salary. I will be better aligned to the company's mission. I will probably work better, if not necessarily harder, because I will not be in a constant state of productivity-sapping anxiety (as discussed in Chapter Three).

From the company's perspective, if I believe my employees are loyal, I am more likely to invest in training. If they stay long enough to absorb the culture, then I can motivate based on the mission, rather than just monetary compensation. And they really may work harder. In an environment of no loyalty, there's a risk that instead the attitude will be, "At-will employees can go above and beyond and get canned anyway, so why bother?"[245]

~~~

I find much to admire in the statement of Saint Ambrose that "no duty is more important than that of returning thanks."[246] Gratitude is not only a moral necessity, but a driver of productivity and social unity.

There are ways to try to create "fake gratitude" – to gain the benefits of reciprocal altruism without any need at all to be altruistic. Non-compete clauses are a popular method, ensuring employees can't take the benefits of their knowledge or training to competitors and thus creating a kind of forced, artificial loyalty. That works to an extent, unless, say, it's banned by the Federal Trade Commission.[247]

---

[245] Borchers, Callum, "The Big Work Lie: Being Indispensable Will Save Your Job," *The Wall Street Journal*, April 3, 2024.
[246] Pope Pius XI, *Quadragesimo Anno*, Encyclical on Reconstruction of the Social Order, 1931.
[247] Federal Trade Commission, "Non-Compete Clause Rule," *16 CFR Part 910*, 2024. While the implementation of the ban was delayed by a federal judge and as of this writing it's unclear whether the FTC will be found to have exceeded its statutory authority, there is considerable legal pressure on non-competes. For example, I understand they are quite difficult to enforce in the state of New York.

Informal rules can also try to restrict employee mobility. When I worked in Chile, the Big Four public accounting firms had an informal rule against staff moving from one to the other, which kept salaries low. I broke it and took two colleagues with me. It's worth noting that the Chilean firms were trying to have it both ways – they frequently dismissed employees at will, but tried to prohibit them from moving voluntarily to competitors.

I believe the better solution is something much more like real gratitude. While I would certainly never advocate for a return to feudal society, there was something to the concept of *noblesse oblige* – the obligation that the powerful (should) feel to those around them.[248] The idea is illustrated in the acclaimed television series Downton Abbey.[249] The Earl of Grantham could have been a very unlikable character. He's a conservative patriarch with all the prejudices of his class. What redeems him is his profound sense of obligation to his staff, the estate's tenant farmers, and the surrounding community. That sense of obligation is on display from the first episode, and makes the character appealing rather than loathsome.[250]

How might we foster a sense of gratitude? I suggest four approaches:

(1) Recognize our mutual interdependence;

(2) Actively endeavor to create group feeling;

(3) Encourage constructive conflict; and

(4) Foster long-term commitment.

Recognizing interdependence requires humility. To a large extent it is countercultural in modern society. The term "independence" has overwhelmingly positive connotations in our world, from the Declaration of Independence as the founding document of the United States to concepts of "financial independence" advocated by investment advisors. Towns are named "Independence." The term is synonymous with autonomy, self-determination, self-sufficiency, sovereignty, and strength. All of those are good things.

---

[248] "Noblesse oblige," Wikimedia Foundation, last modified December 17, 2024, https://en.wikipedia.org/wiki/Noblesse_oblige.
[249] Khalsa, Balihar, "Downton Abbey wins Guinness World Record," *Broadcast Now*, September 13, 2011.
[250] Fellowes, Julian, *Downton Abbey* (PBS, 2010 – 2015).

By contrast, to be dependent on someone sounds bad. Even the Catholic saint who serves as a model of humility, Saint Therese of Lisieux, "dreaded more than anything else, a long illness that would make me a burden to the Community."[251]

We don't like to feel that we owe anyone anything. So it becomes the job of leaders to remind us of our interconnectedness. And not just the call-out to the salesperson who scored the big win this month, which is the usual approach. Every member of the team should feel like they are part of the mission. If they don't feel like that, perhaps they are part of a bureaucracy that isn't performing a useful function and that needs to be reexamined. But if employees who aren't revenue-generating are in fact a useful part of the back office, they should be made to feel that way, and their contribution to the mission should be clear to them and others.

People like to be purpose-driven. In differentiating between the "profane" (the day-to-day behavior of working, eating, and so forth) and the "sacred" (collective search for a higher ideal), Durkheim states:

> *Thus both with the individual and in the group, the faculty of idealizing has nothing mysterious about it. It is not a sort of luxury which a man could get along without, but a condition of his very existence. He could not be a social being, that is to say, he could not be a man, if he had not acquired it.*[252]

People seek meaning in something larger than themselves. Durkheim goes on to concede that even within the realm of the sacred, "in incarnating themselves in individuals, collective ideals tend to individualize themselves." Not only do people put their own "spin" on the greater purpose, but we can fairly suspect from the preceding chapters that spin will be self-interested. As Haidt notes, humans are only 10% bee, and we're 90% chimp. Group feeling will only get you so far – but organizations that don't actively try to create and nourish it will become 100% chimp, with no cooperation beyond what's immediately self-serving.

---

[251] St. Therese of Lisieux, *Story of a Soul*, trans. Thomas N. Taylor (Holy Water Books, 2021), original text 1912, "The Night of the Soul."
[252] Durkheim, *The Elementary Forms of Religious Life*, Conclusion.

To nurture that group feeling in most modern organizations requires buy-in, which in turn requires the opportunity for dissent. True, there are some rigidly hierarchical organizations that by design limit those opportunities. A Catholic priest swears obedience to his bishop. Article 92 of the Uniform Code of Military Justice requires that any lawful order be obeyed.[253] But for most organizations, I agree with Lencioni that constructive conflict is an essential step in building a high-functioning team.

Albert Hirschman in *Exit, Voice, and Loyalty*[254] differentiates between "exit" and "voice" as the two fundamental ways that dissatisfied stakeholders can express themselves. Very simply, "exit" is walking away. It's most common when a buyer decides to switch suppliers because the original supplier increased the price or lowered the quality. The idea of "exit" is the basis for the theory of competition in markets. It also works well in the context of at-will employment. We can leave for something better.

"Voice" is more commonly used in the political sphere. It is quite simply complaining or lobbying to effect change. It is more commonly used in social organizations that are hard to leave, like a country or church. Hirschman argues that voice is under-utilized in the business world, because economists tend to focus on exit. At-will employment reduces voice precisely by empowering exit, either voluntary or involuntary. Hirschman notes that management (or politicians) will often seek to silence those who might annoy them into needed reforms:

> *Expulsion can be interpreted as an instrument – one of many – which "management" uses in these organizations to restrict resort to voice by members.... The importance of loyalty from our point of view is that it can neutralize within certain limits the tendency of the most quality-conscious customers or members to be the first to exit... this tendency deprives the faltering firm or organization of those who could best help it fight its shortcomings and its difficulties.*[255]

---

[253] 10 U.S. Code § 892 - Art. 92. *Failure to obey order or regulation*, 1956.
[254] Hirschman, Albert, *Exit, Voice, and Loyalty* (Harvard University Press, 1970), "Introduction and Doctrinal Background."
[255] Ibid, "A Theory of Loyalty."

Loyalty actually encourages the helpful forms of dissent, because loyal people will try to reform an organization rather than simply abandoning it. But the leaders of those organizations might subtly or unsubtly encourage reformers to leave voluntarily:

> *Those who hold power in the lazy monopoly may actually have an interest in creating some limited opportunities for exit on the part of those whose voice might be uncomfortable.... Latin American powerholders have long encouraged their political enemies to remove themselves from the scene through voluntary exile.*[256]

It's in the interests of an organization for the reform-minded to stick around and make their views known. It may not necessarily be in the interests of those currently in charge, which is why management (or politicians) sometimes finds itself in the position of being disloyal to employees (or voters) and then surprised when the employees (or voters) are disloyal to the organization.

Not every reform proposal is right. But recall Lencioni's and Haidt's observations that a healthy organization includes respectful disagreement and criticism, even if the ultimate conclusion is that no change is needed.

---

[256] Ibid, "How Monopoly Can be Comforted by Competition."

Finally, I believe longevity is a necessary contributor to loyalty. It's true that experiments have found that loyalty to the in-group (and friction with out-groups) can develop very quickly.[257] However, definite commitment to a mission – moving from "I" to "we" – must involve a period of time. For me to even consider putting the group's needs over my own, I have to feel some kind of long-term attachment to the group. Otherwise I'll just go with the flow to be comfortable and advance my status. To be cynical, reciprocal altruism only works if you're going to be part of the group long enough to reap the benefits of the reciprocal exchange. As Robert Conway says in expressing his concerns about the rate of turnover in public accounting, "How can the profession achieve meaningful improvements in audit quality with a work force having such a short-term outlook on their time as a Big Four professional?"[258]

Obvious but left unmentioned above is that simple acts of human kindness can increase loyalty. For many years I worked for a brilliant, hard-charging, workaholic partner who might have been the inspiration for Meryl Streep's character in *The Devil Wears Prada*. It was never too early or too late for a phone call, never too strange a time to jump on a plane to go to a meeting. Nearly twenty years ago I was working in the field on one of the nation's largest telecom mergers, an extremely high-profile, time-sensitive exercise. I got a call late one night from my parents telling me that my father's cancer had recurred. I called my boss to tell him that I needed to leave the field to be with my parents, and that I would try to do as much as I could remotely. His only response was, "Why are you on the phone with me instead of on a plane to your parents' house? We'll take care of the work." I'm still grateful to him.

Yes, gratitude undermines our myth of being entirely self-created, pulled up by our own bootstraps. It implies a sense of obligation to others. We may feel that obligation infringes on our freedom to act as best serves our interests in the moment, and we may resent that limitation on our liberty. I can only offer the words of Edmund Burke:

[257] Sherif, Muzafer, O. J. Harvey, B. Jack White, William R. Hood, Carolyn W. Sherif, *Intergroup Conflict and Cooperation: The Robbers Cave Experiment*, 1954, https://psychclassics.yorku.ca/Sherif/chap7.htm.
[258] Conway, *The Truth About Public Accounting*, "The Truth About Public Accounting at the Staff Level."

But what is liberty without wisdom and without virtue? It is the greatest of all possible evils; for it is folly, vice, and madness, without tuition or restraint.[259]

---

[259] Burke, *Reflections on the Revolution in France.*

...And the Way Forward

"I'm not OK. You're not OK. But it's OK!"

-    Chris Padgett[260]

One of my colleagues likened due diligence to collecting a bag of dead rats. You find an understated liability, an out-of-period adjustment, a bad revenue trend, and they go into the bag. At the end of the project, you plop your bag of dead rats on your client's desk and say, "Look at all the dead rats I found!" But your client doesn't want a bunch of dead rats. They want to know what to do about them – set traps, buy a cat, whatever. They want a solution.

I've just dumped a bag of selfish, jealous, shortsighted, stubborn, ungrateful rats on your desk. I assume you're wondering what to do with them. My problem is that I'm better at finding rats than figuring out what to do about them. As G.K. Chesterton said in this book's opening quote, finding the problem is generally easier than finding the solution. What I will say with a high degree of confidence is that the solution will never be trivially simple.

"Why don't we just...?" may be my least favorite phrase in the English language. It implies that an easy, costless solution is available to... well, I've heard the phrase applied to just about everything. It ranges from solving complex problems in the Middle East to getting people to better assess engagement acceptance risk in a public accounting firm. "Why don't we just add another question on the form?" Of course, the form already contains a hundred questions that no one reads because there are a hundred of them, each one added when someone asked, "Why don't we just add another question on the form?"

[260] Padgett, Chris. *I'm not OK. You're not Ok. But it's OK!* (Wellspring, 2014).

The answer to "Why don't we just..." is usually "Because it's more complicated than you think it is." And while sometimes that complication is technical, frequently it's human. Because people are selfish, jealous, shortsighted, stubborn, and ungrateful. It may well be that the proposed solution would work perfectly if everyone was always selfless, altruistic, visionary, openminded, and loyal. But I haven't met the person yet who is always all of those things. And if they existed, they probably wouldn't be in charge or wouldn't stay that way after they got there. Remember the lessons of Chapter Two about the people who tend to rise to the top.

I found a perfect example of "Why don't we just...?" when I did a Google search on the phrase. After getting past the pop song and boy band, I found *We Could Fix Everything, We Just Don't* by Erik McClure (no relation, as far as I know). Erik believes that most of the world's problems, from cancer to education to bad software coding, could be easily fixed, except that "society is run by people who are incentivized to sabotage cooperation in the name of profits."[261] In other words, society is run by people who are selfish, jealous, shortsighted, stubborn, and ungrateful. The problem is, **that's all of us**.

And even if some of us aren't like that now, we'd almost certainly become like that if we were in charge. I know people who have changed, and not for the better, as they've moved up the hierarchy. There's a reason people keep quoting Lord Acton's line that power tends to corrupt.

As we've seen, it doesn't even matter if the corrupting effects of the power we want so much don't make us happy. As Wright notes:

> *The essence of addiction, after all, is that pleasure tends to dissipate and leave the mind agitated, hungry for more. The idea that just one more dollar, one more dalliance, one more rung on the ladder will leave us feeling sated reflects a misunderstanding about human nature – a misunderstanding, moreover, that is built into human nature.*[262]

[261] https://erikmcclure.com/blog/we-could-fix-everything-we-just-dont/.
[262] Wright, *The Moral Animal*, "Darwin Gets Religion."

We act in obnoxious ways just because that's how we are, and we make up a justification later. Take what is perhaps the best known case study of selfishness and betrayal, the passion of Jesus. We don't need to engage with the theological aspects; it's well accepted in academic circles that Jesus was a historical person who was crucified.[263] The basic elements of that story, then, are that a prominent preacher was betrayed by one of his own closest followers, handed over to the Roman authorities, and executed by those authorities in a particularly humiliating, agonizing manner for actions that were not crimes under Roman law.

What happened there? Did Judas betray Jesus for money or to save his own skin (which didn't work out well, since he's then understood to have killed himself),[264] or was he jealous that he wasn't one of the three most favored disciples (John, James, and Peter)? Did the Jewish leaders resent Jesus' challenge to their authority, or were they concerned that the Romans might view him as a threat and destroy the Temple?[265] What exactly was going through Pontius Pilate's mind when he decided to execute someone he had determined was innocent because he was afraid of unrest? Whatever the exact motivations of the participants, no one comes out looking good. Even Peter, the greatest of the apostles, denies knowing Jesus three times.

---

[263] "Historicity of Jesus," Wikimedia Foundation, last modified January 21, 2025, https://en.wikipedia.org/wiki/Historicity_of_Jesus.
[264] Matthew 27:5.
[265] John 11:47-50.

We'd surely like to think we've gotten better than that. And in some ways we probably have. Over the intervening millennia there have been many positive moral developments. Enlightened people no longer accept slavery, racism, sexism, or sexual violence. On the other hand, we come back to Milgram's infamous 1961 experiment[266] in which, responding to the authority of the experimenter, 65% of subjects assigned to an "instructor" role administered to a "learner" what they (falsely) believed to be an electrical shock at a level labeled as beyond "dangerous."[267] Christianity, a religion based on two "great commandments" one of which is "love your neighbor as yourself,"[268] gave us the Spanish Inquisition, the Crusades, and the European Wars of Religion. Marx's promotion of the good of the masses gave us famines, the gulag, the Cultural Revolution, and Cambodia's Killing Fields. Effective altruism gave us Sam Bankman-Fried at FTX.

My observation is that we see selfishness, jealousy, shortsightedness, stubbornness, and ingratitude in every human institution. That's true of private companies, public accounting firms, governments, non-profits, churches, you name it. No matter how noble the mission, people are still people – a strong sense of mission can help mitigate some of the perversities of egoism, but never all of them. Indeed, most traditions, whether Western or Eastern, hold that very few individuals ever achieve detachment from their selfish desires, even if they're diligently seeking it. Saint John of the Cross says that there are very few who pass fully through the dark night of the soul to complete spiritual purgation, so as to pass fully "through the narrow gate"[269] – he also says the process is intensely painful.[270]

---

[266] Milgram, Stanley, "Behavioral Study of Obedience," *Journal of Abnormal and Social Psychology 67(4)*, 1963.

[267] This finding shocked (so to speak) the research community, which had predicted that only 1% or so of respondents would deliver the highest level shock. Brennan in *Business Ethics for Better Behavior*, "Psychological Factors," challenges whether this finding represents self-interest on the part of the "instructor" who is the subject of the experiment. I believe it does, and specifically addresses the topic of jealousy. The experimenter was perceived to have social power over the subject in this setting. Because humans are subject to social hierarchy, we have a strong incentive to obey those who are designated as our superiors in a particular situation, so as not to lose status within the group.

[268] Mark 12:31.

[269] Matthew 7:13.

[270] San Juan de la Cruz, *Noche Oscura del Alma* (Ivory Falls Books, 2017), original text 16th Century, Ch.8.

By this point, you're hopefully persuaded that the ordinary human being tends to be selfish, jealous, shortsighted, stubborn, and ungrateful. Maybe you don't believe me, but if so, I would respectfully suggest that maybe you're not paying attention not just to what you've read, but also to the world you observe around you. As Steven Pinker wryly observes as he explains the evolutionary basis for jealousy, infidelity, and war:

> *No one needs a scientist to measure whether humans are*
> *prone to knavery. The question has been answered in the*
> *history books, the newspapers, the ethnographic record, and*
> *the letters to Ann Landers.*[271]

I'm not saying everyone is a sociopath like Bernie Madoff. Nor am I denying the existence of saints like Mother Teresa of Calcutta. What I'm saying is that, by biological design and in easily observable behavior, ordinary people like you and me tend to look out for ourselves in fairly predictable ways. And sometimes those behaviors have unfortunate consequences for us and for those around us.

Then again, maybe I'm wrong. Brennan asserts that in most cases, ethically unfortunate actions don't arise from deliberate bad behavior:

> *Neither of these are the kinds of behaviors that*
> *stereotypically selfish, greedy, and confident people engage*
> *in... Our claim is that most wrong-doing in business is not a*
> *result of selfish people choosing to be selfish over being*
> *morally good.*[272]

Brennan cites many of the same sources that I do, including Ariely, Bazerman, Milgram, and the Enron debacle. So it's very interesting that he looks at the same evidence and seems to be coming to almost exactly the opposite conclusion.

Except I don't think he is. Brennan says:

---

[271] Pinker, *How the Mind Works*, "Family Values."
[272] Brennan, English, Hasnas, and Jaworski, *Business Ethics for Better Behavior*, "Psychological Factors."

Whereas others are going to be tempted by power, status, and money, this won't happen to you. You are, after all, a good person, who heeds the angel on your left shoulder and disregards the devil on your right shoulder. If you think this, then you are, once again, engaged in self-flattery... It is not that we look to the devil sitting on our left shoulder and choose him over the angel perched on our other shoulder. Instead, we look straight ahead, never noticing the devil nor the angel at all.[273]

I think Brennan is saying the same thing I am, in a different way. It's not that most of us are choosing to act wrongly, or that we are sociopaths who don't even understand the difference between right and wrong. We aren't waking up one morning and deliberately deciding to betray employees with decades of service by offshoring their jobs, or putting customers at risk by cutting back on safety inspections. Instead, we're subject to a kind of incentive-driven moral blindness.

As Bazerman says:

Ethics training presumes that emphasizing the moral components of decisions will inspire executives to choose the moral path. But the common assumption this training is based on – that executives make explicit trade-offs between behaving ethically and earning profits for their organizations – is incomplete. This paradigm fails to acknowledge our innate psychological responses when faced with an ethical dilemma... the more pernicious aspect of conflicts of interest is clarified by well-replicated research showing that when people have a vested interest in seeing a problem in a certain manner, they are no longer capable of objectivity.[274]

We behave in selfish, jealous, shortsighted, stubborn, and ungrateful ways not because we consciously choose to, but because as human beings we're wired that way.

---

[273] Ibid.

[274] Bazerman and Tenbrunsel, *Blind Spots*, "The Gap between Intended and Actual Ethical Behavior."

Let's say you believe me. The next logical question is, "So what?" If we accept those truths about human nature, are we doomed "to a life of skepticism, indecision, disgust, and often misanthropy"[275]? Edmund Burke warned of this risk. "By hating vices too much, they come to love men too little. It is, therefore, not wonderful that they should be indisposed and unable to serve them."[276] Should we conclude that because human beings are neither perfect nor perfectible, there's nothing to be done? Should we despise our fellow human beings because they're flawed? In other words, do we just throw up our hands and conclude, "People suck"?

I don't think so. The point is not to hate ourselves because we're flawed, but simply to acknowledge and accept that we're flawed.[277] It's true that humans suffer greatly, largely at our own hands. And I must admit that I struggle a bit with the Dalai Lama's view that humans **are** basically gentle, although I agree with him that we **should be**. But the Dalai Lama takes what I view as a very realistic and productive approach to the inevitability of suffering, and how we should approach it:

> *If we think of suffering as unnatural, something that we shouldn't be experiencing, then it's not much of a leap to look for someone to blame for our suffering... But as long as we view suffering as an unnatural state, an abnormal condition that we fear, avoid, and reject, we will never uproot the causes of suffering and begin to live a happier life.*[278]

---

[275] Shklar, *Ordinary Vices*, "Putting Cruelty First."

[276] Burke, *Reflections on the Revolution in France.*

[277] Pope Benedict XVI went so far as to say in *In the Beginning...* "A selflessness that tries to abolish one's own 'I' degenerates into 'I-lessness,' and then 'Thou-lessness' follows directly. This undermining of creation can never become a vehicle of grace, but only of an *odium generis humani...*"

[278] HH Dalai Lama and Cutler, *The Art of Happiness*, "Facing Suffering."

Suffering, including that caused by the deliberate or negligent acts of others, is a natural part of the human experience. Here I tend to subscribe to the approach of Thomas Sowell. Sowell is sort of the modern equivalent of Edmund Burke – his worldview could perhaps be summarized as, "You're not as smart as you think you are." And given that Sowell himself is very smart, I'm inclined to believe him. He argues for a "constrained vision," one which acknowledges the limitations and fallibility of all human beings and the recognition that humans cannot be perfected in this world. However, he clearly states that, "The constrained vision was not synonymous with (or camouflage for) acceptance of the status quo."[279]

The view that humans aren't perfect or perfectible does not mean no improvement is possible. Not only would that conclusion be profoundly pessimistic, it would be unrealistic. We have, after all, greatly reduced the social acceptability of many kinds of awful behavior. No moral guide, from Jesus to Buddha, would have bothered if humans weren't capable of receiving moral guidance. Instead, we need to seek realistic solutions that consider the nature of our raw material (humans), while acknowledging the limitations of what we can accomplish. As Friedrich Hayek observed about central planning:

> *It is important not to confuse opposition against this kind of planning with a dogmatic laissez faire attitude. The liberal argument is in favor of making the best possible uses of competition as a means of coordinating human efforts, not an argument for leaving things just as they are.*[280]

Hirschman has a similar observation. People will manipulate even the best of institutions for their own ends. Our task, like that of the founding fathers of the United States, is to devise systems that mitigate as much as possible the effects of those manipulations. And then to address the corruption of those institutions as it invariably creeps in.

---

[279] Sowell, *A Conflict of Visions*, "The Mobilization of Knowledge."
[280] Hayek, Friedrich, *The Road to Serfdom*, ed. By Bruce Caldwell (University of Chicago Press, 2007), original text 1944, "Individualism and Collectivism."

> *Under any economic, social, or political system, individuals,*
> *business firms, and organizations in general are subject to*
> *lapses from efficient, rational, law-abiding, virtuous, or*
> *otherwise functional behavior. No matter how well a*
> *society's basic institutions are devised, failures of some*
> *actors to live up to the behavior which is expected of them*
> *are bound to occur, if only for all kinds of accidental*
> *reasons. Each society learns to live with a certain amount of*
> *such dysfunctional or misbehavior; but lest the misbehavior*
> *feed on itself and lead to general decay, society must be able*
> *to marshal from within itself forces which will make as many*
> *of the faltering actors as possible revert to the behavior*
> *required for its proper functioning.*[281]

My only modification to Hirschman's view would be to suggest that not just "some," but almost every actor is prone to some level of misbehavior, if we define "misbehavior" as being selfish, jealous, shortsighted, stubborn, and ungrateful.

Depressingly, every mitigation contains the seeds of its own corruption. Sowell notes:

> *In the unconstrained vision, there are no intractable reasons*
> *for social evils and therefore no reason why they cannot be*
> *solved, with sufficient moral commitment. But in the*
> *constrained vision, whatever artifices or strategies restrain*
> *or ameliorate inherent human evils will themselves have*
> *costs.*[282]

We should thus be realistic both about the need for reform and the scope of what it can accomplish. As Edmund Burke summarized, "We cannot change the Nature of things and of men – but must act upon them the best we can."[283]

---

[281] Hirschman, *Exit, Voice, and Loyalty*, "Introduction and Doctrinal Background."
[282] Sowell, *A Conflict of Visions*, "Social Morality and Social Causation."
[283] Thomas Sowell in *A Conflict of Visions* credits this statement to Edmund Burke in Volume VI of his *Correspondence*. I can't find the quote in my abridged copy of Burke's works or another readily available source, but not all of Burke's writings are readily available and I'm inclined to take Sowell's word for it.

Ibn Khaldun puts it even more bluntly: "Injustice is a human trait. If you find a moral man, there is some reason why he is not unjust."[284]

The question, then, is how do we act upon selfish, jealous, shortsighted, stubborn, and ungrateful humans, to give them reasons not to be unjust? Again, realism doesn't mean fatalistic acceptance of human misbehavior, or misanthropic dislike for our fellow humans. Being realistic about human nature doesn't necessarily mean we can mitigate all of the resulting problems; but being unrealistic almost guarantees we can't.

An instructively horrifying example of reform not just failing but consuming itself was Robespierre's Reign of Terror in the French Revolution, which culminated with the execution of Robespierre himself. The same abuses occurred in the Russian Revolution, and can be observed today in Venezuela, where the understandable desire to reduce the power of the existing oligarchy resulted instead in a repressive, incompetent dictatorship. If you give people unlimited power, they'll probably use it. Probably in bad ways. For every Lee Kuan Yew there are dozens of Vladimir Putins, Nicolas Maduros, and Kim Jong Uns who cling to power like a cat with its claws sunk into the carpet, immiserating the citizens they allegedly serve.

If we are to have reform, it must be not just realistic, but also compassionate. Chesterton says:

> *The optimist is a better reformer than the pessimist.... There is a great man who makes every man feel small. But the real great man is the man who makes every man feel great.*[285]

---

[284] Ibn Khaldun, *The Muqaddimah*, Ch.2.
[285] Chesterton, G.K., *Collected Works of G.K. Chesterton* (Delphi Classics, 2014), original text 1906, "Charles Dickens: A Critical Study."

My own view of the key to success has evolved over time. As I mentioned in the fourth chapter, I obtained just about every academic honor obtainable. I don't labor under a lot of false modesty – I think I'm pretty smart. Early in my career, I would have said intelligence was the key to success. Later on, I changed that criterion to reliability – getting done what I said I'd get done. Later still, I favored adaptability – being willing and able to handle the curve balls that life threw at me. But at this point in my life, I'd say the key is compassion.[286] It's understanding the motivations and frailties of those around me, seeing them reflected in myself, and trying to act with empathy.

Throughout this book I may not have seemed like Chesterton's optimistic reformer. I've deliberately used provocative language with negative connotations to describe human behavior. What if instead I suggested that we want things to go according to our plans, to be respected, to enjoy the things that give us pleasure, to be consistent, and to be free from societal constraints? None of those sound bad. But all I did was to put a more positive spin on being selfish, jealous, shortsighted, stubborn, and ungrateful. It's easy to see behaviors as evil in others, especially if those behaviors harm us. It's harder to see the same behaviors as evil in ourselves.

---

[286] I apparently share that view with the Dalai Lama, see for example the chapter "The Value and Benefits of Compassion" in *The Art of Happiness* by HH Dalai Lama and Cutler. Let me hasten to state that doesn't mean I'm enlightened – it's probably more like the blind squirrel occasionally finding a nut.

We always tend to see the splinter in our brother's eye and ignore the log in our own.[287] I tell my catechism students that in my mind, whenever Jesus is talking to the Pharisees in the Gospels, he's talking to me and people like me – people who go to church every week, think we're trying to do the right thing, and run the risk of judging others. The easy interpretation of the story of the prodigal son is that it's aimed at the younger son, who runs off and misbehaves, and then is welcomed back. But in context, it's clearly directed even more at the older son, who stands in for the Pharisees – the one who stayed close to the father, and is judgmental and jealous because his good-for-nothing brother gets welcomed home.[288] The younger son is guilty of the lower sins of the flesh. The older son is guilty of the higher sin of pride. People who are reading this book (as well as the guy who wrote it) are more likely to be the older son.

There's a temptation if we think we're better than everyone else to try to impose our will on them. The better option is a quieter, more humble one. As Edmund Burke says, "Our patience will achieve more than our force."[289]

Peter, the most famously rash, violent, pig-headed, and generally obnoxious of Jesus' apostles, seemed to finally mellow with age (and the inspiration of the Holy Spirit) and framed reform in terms of respectful optimism:

> *Always be ready to make your defense to anyone who*
> *demands from you an accounting for the hope that is in you;*
> *yet do it with gentleness and reverence.*[290]

~~~

So what do concrete steps to mitigate selfishness, jealousy, shortsightedness, stubbornness, and ingratitude look like? If we simply compile the recommendations from the previous five chapters, we have this:

I.   Selfish – establish culture with real rules that:

(1) People talk about all the time;

---

[287] Matthew 7:3.
[288] Luke 15:1-32. The parable of the prodigal son is contained in Luke 15:11-32, but Luke 15:1-2 sets the stage that Jesus is addressing the Pharisees, who are angry that he associates with sinners and tax collectors.
[289] Burke, *Reflections on the Revolution in France.*
[290] 1 Peter 3:15-16.

(2) People are rewarded for following;

(3) People are punished for not following; and

(4) Are easy to follow thanks to robust systems and processes.

II. Jealous – to minimize "winner takes all":

(1) Limit the scope of control;

(2) Don't pit people against each other;

(3) Align the interests of the governing and the governed; and

(4) Use oversight to check absolute power.

III. Shortsighted – to help people do the right thing:

(1) Engage the emotions in a positive rather than punitive way;

(2) Use input and feedback to test the resonance of messaging;

(3) Limit compliance tasks to the essential; and

(4) Give people the tools to achieve compliance.

IV. Stubborn – to counter extremism and bureaucracy:

(1) Approach every issue with intellectual humility;

(2) Encourage respectful dissent;

(3) Take a fact-based approach to problem solving; and

(4) Understand that the ends generally don't justify the means.

V. Ungrateful – to create solidarity:

(1) Recognize our mutual interdependence;

(2) Actively endeavor to create group feeling;

(3) Encourage constructive conflict; and

(4) Foster long-term commitment.

That's quite a list, and there's an inherent tension between some of the recommendations. For example, I talk about the need for rewards and punishments to establish culture, but I also talk about not pitting people against each other or engaging the emotions in a fear-based way. Loyalty and group feeling are important, but in-group dynamics can spiral into nepotism and discrimination. These topics are difficult.

Reflecting on it, I condense the recommendations down to four very broad proposals:

1. Engage with humility, respect for dissent, and reliance on data.

2. Foster a sense of mission and community supported by intrinsic, understandable rules.

3. Limit the scope of control with minimal concentrations of power.

4. Make compliance easy, backed up with appropriate incentives.

Humility, dissent, and data

Why do I start with humility? Beginning with mission felt more natural in many ways. But humility is one of those virtues that is widely revered in spiritual teachings, yet widely rejected by our society. The Bible says, "Blessed are the meek, for they will inherit the earth."[291] The Tao says, "If you are brave but lack compassion, are generous but lack economy, and try to help but lack humility, you've lost the way."[292] And yet we are constantly told to emphasize who we know, what we know, and what we've accomplished. Just look at LinkedIn. The Litany of Humility and the Eight Verses on the Training of the Mind are not just *hard*, but countercultural.

The scientific method was supposed to make us humble. In science, there is no revealed truth. There are hypotheses and the testing of hypotheses. In most religions, there is some form of revealed truth, but that revelation differs based on the particular faith. My view is that there is a Truth, but we must be free to find it, and humble enough to accept that we need to keep seeking it. I agree with Alan Bloom:

---

[291] Matthew 5:5.
[292] Lao Tzu, *Tao Te Ching*, "Compassion."

The real community of man, in the midst of all the self-contradictory simulacra of community, is the community of those who seek the truth... Their common concern for the good linked them; their disagreement about it proved they needed one another to understand it.[293]

One of the most commonly cited passages from the Quran is, "Let there be no compulsion in religion." That is not because Muslims believe that there is ambiguity as to whether or not the teachings of Islam are true. In fact, the reference reads more fully, "Let there be no compulsion in religion, for the truth stands out clearly from falsehood."[294]

Compulsion isn't prohibited because the topic is unimportant, or because Muslims believe there are multiple valid options. Rather, the answer is too important to make acquiescence compulsory. People need to assess the facts and arrive at their own conclusions. That is the benefit of both the economic marketplace and the marketplace of ideas. Different views of the truth can be aired, tested, and decided upon – even in our current age of misinformation and disinformation. As Haidt and Lencioni highlight, that is why constructive conflict is necessary.

---

[293] Bloom, *The Closing of the American Mind*, "The Student and the University." Mirroring this concept, in *The Abolition of Man* (HarperCollins, 2009, original text 1944), C.S. Lewis refers to this multi-faith search for the absolute truth as "the Tao" (despite being a Christian) and characterizes it as variously "Natural Law or Traditional Morality or the First Principles of Practical Reason or the First Platitudes" that is "the sole source of all value judgments."
[294] Al-Baqarah 256.

Frequently there are two (or more) competing theories of what will be helpful in a particular case. For example, studies by Bazerman and his colleagues show that people maintain a "moral equilibrium." If they are asked do things that make them regard themselves as honest (like contemplate all the great things they've done), they then give themselves more latitude to do the wrong thing in a gray area while maintaining their moral self-image.[295] By contrast, work by Ariely and his colleagues show if people are asked to do things that make them regard themselves as *dishonest* (like wearing fake designer sunglasses), they then give themselves more latitude to do the wrong thing in a gray area while maintaining their moral self-image.[296] Ironically, one researcher worked on both the studies that seem to yield a contradictory result.

While both hypotheses appear plausible, it doesn't seem like those two conclusions can both be right. Maybe they are both right, and there's some nuance to the psychology that produces seemingly contradictory results based on slight differences in the situations. Maybe they're both wrong, and regarding yourself as honest or dishonest doesn't actually produce any effect, and the conclusions simply result from p-hacking[297] or some other testing error. I don't know. The point is that plausible hypotheses, even those supported by testing, can still be wrong.[298]

---

[295] Bazerman and Tenbrunsel, *Blind Spots*, "Placing False Hope in the 'Ethical Organization.'"

[296] Ariely, *The Honest Truth About Dishonesty*, "Why Wearing Fakes Makes Us Cheat More."

[297] *P*-hacking results from the fact that if you run enough experiments, you will eventually get an outcome that looks statistically significant just due to random chance. In the most bizarre case of this effect that I ever saw, I watched a friend of mine repeatedly roll ten dice that eventually came up all sixes, which has a one-in-sixty-million probability of occurring; he didn't roll the dice anything like sixty million times, but I suppose it had to happen to someone somewhere. Michael Kearns and Aaron Roth provide an excellent discussion of *p*-hacking in *The Ethical Algorithm*, "Lost in the Garden: Led Astray by Data" (Oxford University Press, 2019).

[298] For what it's worth, I'm tentatively inclined towards Bazerman's "moral equilibrium" hypothesis. I've observed that if I buy my wife an expensive handbag on Fifth Avenue, I tend to give a big donation to the next homeless person I see to make up for having blown a lot of money on an unnecessary luxury. On the other hand, you could make a plausible counterargument that being generous to my wife makes me feel generous towards others. There is a frightening way of squaring this circle, which is that perhaps people can use *any* external variable as a way to rationalize bad behavior. That hypothesis would be consistent with Ariely (*The Honest Truth About Dishonesty*, "Creativity and Dishonesty) and Haidt (*The Righteous Mind*, "Intuitions Come First, Strategic Reasoning Second") who maintain that to some extent our concept of morality (at least applied to ourselves) consists of rationalizations. Give someone a new factor to play with, whatever that factor may be, and they can use it to rationalize a decision they might not have otherwise felt comfortable with.

Maybe the compliance intervention I mentioned in the fourth chapter really wasn't responsible for the observed improvement, although the effect was incredibly strong and replicated across multiple trials. The fact that I didn't like that particular intervention helps me believe it really was helpful, since I didn't have any bias towards wanting it to work.

Being humble, respectful, and data-driven means being open to new approaches – mitigating the danger of bureaucracy. But it also means accepting that innovation may cause unanticipated problems, or not work out as intended – mitigating the danger of extremism. Being data-driven can lead to innovation, but it can also support traditionalism. As Sowell says, "Rules, traditions, and self-discipline all represent guidance from the distilled experiences of others, rather than self-indulgence based on the inner light of one's one vision."[299]

We should remember that, as flawed as current structures may be, they have worked well enough to get our society where it is. I've cited ancient texts, many of them religious, throughout this book, not to proselytize, but because their durability strongly suggests they have something valuable to say. As Robert Wright puts it, applying evolutionary theory to religious practice:

> *Does this mean common religious teachings have some sort of timeless value as rules to live by? Donald T. Campell, one of the first psychologists to get enthusiastic about modern Darwinism, has suggested as much. In an address to the American Psychological Association, he spoke of "the possible sources of validity in recipes for living that have been evolved, tested, and winnowed through hundreds of generations of human social history. On purely scientific grounds, these recipes for living might be regarded as better tested than the best of psychology's and psychiatry's speculations on how lives should be lived.[300]*

---

[299] Sowell, *The Quest for Cosmic Justice.*
[300] Wright, *The Moral Animal*, "Darwin Gets Religion.".

And one of the great virtues of common religious teachings is their emphasis on humility. Numerous theologians have pointed out that humility is simply realism.[301] We are each very small things in the universe. Our understanding is limited. Our moral judgment is flawed. We don't always know the right thing to do, or do it when we know it. Walter Ciszek, a Catholic priest who was imprisoned in the Soviet gulag for fifteen years following five years in solitary confinement, defined spiritual freedom as surrendering your will to God, but wrote, "Spiritual freedom of this sort, as I knew from bitter experience, is not something that can be attained overnight or ever be possessed in its final form."[302]

In every Catholic Mass, the congregation says, "Lord, I am not worthy that you should enter under my roof."[303] One of my partners, named Kath, told me she didn't like that part of the Mass because it made her feel bad about herself. I told her that was the point. Since she didn't like that answer, I facetiously suggested she could start her own religion called Katholicism that just encouraged you to feel good about yourself.[304] I think most of us are really Katholics. We like to feel good about ourselves and we don't like things that make us question ourselves.

---

[301] For example, Ibn Khaldun says, "God's creation extends beyond the creation of man. Complete knowledge does not exist in man. The world of existence is too vast for him." (Ibn Khaldun, *The Muqaddimah*, Prefatory Discussion.)

[302] Ciszek, Walter, S.J., *He Leadeth Me*, (Crown Publishing, 1973), "Freedom."

[303] Adapted from Matthew 8:8.

[304] Kath's alternative language is actually pretty good, but you'll have to wait for her book to see it.

But questioning ourselves and truly acting with humility is necessary for reform. Otherwise we are just bureaucrats, unable to see any flaws in the system, or extremists, screaming about other people's flaws while overlooking our own. Humility means having an open mind, and at the same time "taming the tongue"[305] to avoid badmouthing others. In the wake of the most horrific war fought on U.S. soil over the defining stain on America's soul, President Lincoln's second inaugural address closed with the humble request "let us judge not that we be not judged... with malice toward none with charity for all."[306] While the sin of slavery had to be paid in blood, Lincoln called for mercy towards those on the wrong side. As a newly ordained priest recently said to me on the subject of humility, gratitude, and mercy, "You'd better be a shining example of that mercy, or you're worse than those that don't know any better."[307]

Mission and community

You may say that it's all very well to be data-driven and act with humility in getting where we're trying to go... but where are we trying to go?

I would suggest we're trying to give people a sense of mission, community, and belonging, to achieve what Emile Durkheim might call "sacred" and Michael Sandel might call "non-market value." It's an elevation above the day-to-day feeding of the wallet, mouth, and ego, to belong to a "we" that is bigger than the "I."

---

[305] James 3:7.
[306] Lincoln, Abraham, *Second Inaugural Address*, 1865.
[307] Father Gregory Zingler, conversation at St. Augustine Roman Catholic Church of Newark, NJ, June 20, 2024.

I've long made the sarcastic remark that people in public accounting are coin-operated. To an extent it's probably true. At least when I was in school, before the 150-hour requirement to sit for the CPA exam, being an accountant was an economically efficient way to make a good living. In the public accounting profession your salary would go up pretty steadily, eventually taking you into affluence as a partner. The joke about accountants is that if you ask us what two plus two is, we'll ask what you want it to be. But as Paul Munter points out, there's something much greater to the profession, or at least there's supposed to be. Being a CPA means that you're committed to telling the truth. You pledge to serve the public interest and to practice with integrity, objectivity and independence, and due care.[308] At our best, there are values that CPAs cannot exchange for money, no matter the cost/benefit tradeoff. Those kinds of values are what Sandel views as being potentially corrupted by market economics, because "market values are corrosive of certain goods but appropriate to others."[309]

An organization (political, religious, social, or economic) that inspires those values, and that sense of mission, is bigger than the individuals that comprise it. Robert Bellah argued, and it is generally accepted, that the United States historically had a kind of "civil religion" which "from the earliest years of the republic is a collection of beliefs, symbols, and rituals with respect to sacred things and institutionalized in a collectivity."[310] It is the unifying notion behind the American idea of "We the people."[311] One might argue – as Sandel does – that monetization is corrupting civil society, robbing it of the sacred.

> *A market **economy** is a tool – a valuable and effective tool – for organizing productive activity. A market **society** is a way of life in which market values seep into every aspect of human endeavor [my emphasis]. It's a place where social relations are made over in the image of the market.[312]*

---

[308] AICPA Code of Professional Conduct Sections 0.0300.030, 040, 050, and 060.
[309] Sandel, *What Money Can't Buy* "Jumping the Queue."
[310] Bellah, Robert, "Civil Religion in America," *Daedalus Journal of the American Academy of Arts and Sciences (96)*, Winter 1967.
[311] Preamble to the United States Constitution, 1787.
[312] Sandel, *What Money Can't Buy*, "Introduction: Markets and Morals."

To use Durkheim's phraseology, it's a world where nothing is sacred, everything is profane. The risk of such a world is in Alan Bloom's words that "In the absence of a common good or common object, as Rousseau puts it, the disintegration of society into particular wills is inevitable."[313]

Bloom goes on to highlight what happens when the society disintegrates into those particular wills:

> *For us the most revealing and delightful distinction –*
> *because it is so unconscious of its wickedness – is between*
> *inner-directed and other-directed, with the former taken to*
> *be unqualifiedly good. Of course, we are told, the healthy*
> *inner-directed person will really care for others. To which I*
> *can only respond: If you can believe that, you can believe*
> *anything.*[314]

C.S. Lewis was even more blunt: "When all that says 'it's good' has been debunked, what says 'I want' remains."[315]

Somewhere at the intersection of Bloom, Deneen, Lewis, and Sandel sits an idea that too much of life has been taken out of the realm of the sacred into the realm of the profane. Too much is about "I," and not enough is about "we." Too much is driven by the choices of the market that carry no moral weight, and not enough by norms of loyalty and decency. Too many relationships, from family to church to employment, are throwaway – not subject to any more loyalty than changing the brand of cereal we eat. We are not willing to place any constraints on our individual choices or self-interest in order to serve a higher cause. In Deneen's framing, "As a result, superficially self-maximizing, socially destructive behaviors begin to dominate society."[316]

In the Bible, Saint Peter put the seductive option of limitless individual choice this way:

---

[313] Bloom, *The Closing of the American Mind*, "Relationships."
[314] Ibid, "Values."
[315] Lewis, *The Abolition of Man*.
[316] Deneen, *Why Liberalism Failed*, "Unsustainable Liberalism." Again, it's important to note that Deneen is pointing to both "left liberalism" (limited social constraints on individual behavior, with state constraints on the market), as well as "right liberalism" (limited constraints on the market, with state constraints on social behavior) as being equally "liberal" and equally problematic.

> *They promise them freedom, but they themselves are slaves*
> *of corruption; for people are slaves to whatever masters*
> *them.*[317]

As I mentioned above, Brennan pushes back on the idea that people are selfish and that selfishness is the main driver of social dysfunction. He says, "The thought that people are motivated primarily by selfishness, and that most bad behavior is the result of too much selfishness, is probably false."[318] I think Brennan means selfishness in the sense of lying, or stealing, or deliberately stepping on others to get ahead. I don't do any of those things. But I'm still quite selfish because I really like to get my own way. I have huge difficulty really meaning the Litany of Humility. When I say, "Lord let me know your will so I may do it," what I really mean is, "Lord let me know what you want me to do within the constraints of my desired lifestyle." What Bloom, Deneen, Lewis, Sandel, and Saint Peter are saying is that I'm not free, because I'm a slave to my own desires. In Haidt's framing of "moral modules," I may be kind and fair, but like many people in modern western society I may be ignoring the moral dimensions of loyalty, authority, and sanctity[319] – which are dimensions that make "I" subordinate to "we."

A sense of mission and community helps us make that transition from "I" to "we." An organization (political, religious, or economic) that creates a binding sense of community lowers the risk of selfish behavior. Community isn't a panacea even if it works – fascists, theocracies, and suicidal cults can all have strong senses of community. So while it is critically important that the organization *have* values, it's also important that the values be good ones. In my organization, we thought a lot about "can versus should." Something that we "can" do is legal and within our technical competency. Something that we "should" do is also consistent with our ethics, mission, and brand. Not everything that we can do is something that we should do.

---

[317] 2 Peter 2:19.
[318] Brennan, English, Hasnas, and Jaworski, *Business Ethics for Better Behavior*, "Psychological Factors."
[319] Haidt, *The Righteous Mind*, "Taste Buds of the Righteous Mind."

I encountered an example in a project I performed before becoming a partner. We were engaged to perform financial due diligence on a company. Financial due diligence is much like an audit, but the procedures are agreed in advance with the client, and only the client can rely on our work. Under the AICPA Code, an audit is a "general distribution report" that can be used by anyone because it has a standard scope of procedures, whereas due diligence is a "limited distribution report" that can only be used by the client with whom the procedures were agreed. However, it's common for the client in a due diligence engagement, generally the purchaser in a mergers and acquisitions transaction, to share the report with its lenders.

In this case, I noted in the report that I believed the target company would soon face competition from a large, aggressive competitor that was emerging from bankruptcy. That created a commercial risk to the target's future revenue projections. My client asked me to remove that observation before sharing the report with the lenders. I objected. The client pointed out that my scope was financial due diligence, not commercial due diligence, so my observation wasn't part of what they'd asked me to do – which was true. The client also noted that I had no duty of care to the lenders and our transmittal letter to the lenders was very explicit about that fact – which was also true. In the end I took the language out. I still don't feel great about it twenty years later. When I became the quality leader for the transaction advisory practice, I tried to deal with the situation by requiring that any information redacted from a report provided to the lenders be specifically noted as such.[320] That seemed like something we "should" do even though it wasn't required by law or regulation.

Even in the famously cutthroat world of mergers and acquisitions where I spent much of my time, buyers and sellers are coming to realize that a sense of mission makes a difference:

---

[320] Max Bazerman might not be very impressed with my solution. He notes that disclosure of conflicts of interest doesn't seem to produce the intended results, which is a little disturbing to me as I also ran the global conflicts of interest function and (per AICPA guidance) we relied very heavily on disclosure. See Bazerman and Tenbrunsel, *Blind Spots*, "Placing False Hope in the 'Ethical Organization.'"

> *For example, in an economy where skilled workers are*
> *scarce resources, a strong relationship with employees*
> *stands as a distinguishing factor for buyers seeking stability*
> *in the workforce. Other examples include a reputation for*
> *collaboration with the supply chain, a reputation for quality*
> *and well-known customer service.[321]*

That doesn't seem to stop many organizations from being ruthless in their pursuit of profits through layoffs, especially larger ones. That may make sense. It's likely harder to maintain mission and community in a larger, more diverse group. Humans are inherently tribal. Jesus asked us to love everyone:

> *You have heard that it was said, You shall love your*
> *neighbor and hate your enemy. But I say to you, love your*
> *enemies and pray for those who persecute you... So be*
> *perfect, just as your heavenly Father is perfect.[322]*

Caring for everyone equally is of course exactly the right sentiment. However, Jesus explicitly notes that it requires perfection, which is elusive. The reality is that our ability to be loyal to other people is limited. As Haidt points out, people with a strong moral orientation towards loyalty tend to have a more particular view of loyalty (to a small group) rather than a universal view of loyalty (to a larger group).[323] It makes sense that it would simply be harder to feel a strong sense of community with a large, diverse group.

The Catholic Church has a practical approach that it's developed over a two thousand year history and applied to over a billion adherents worldwide. Although Catholicism is famously hierarchical with a single supreme authority, it has many smaller, diverse communities within it. There are the Missionaries of Charity, the Jesuits, the Neocatechumenal Way, Opus Dei, and many other charisms within the church. I can attest to the loyalty that some of those groups inspire. Those smaller groups, with their intense loyalty, roll up into the larger Catholic community.

---

[321] Crankshaw, Brooks, "Beyond Numbers: The Unseen Power of Corporate Culture in M&A Transactions," *Forbes Partners*, June 8, 2024, **https://forbes-partners.com/beyond-numbers-the-unseen-power-of-corporate-culture-in-ma-transactions/**.
[322] Matthew 5:43-44, 48.
[323] Haidt, *The Righteous Mind*, "The Moral Foundations of Politics."

Community matters not just to the group as a whole – it matters to the individuals. Multiple studies show that civic engagement is positively correlated with happiness.[324] Strong community connections and a sense of mission are good for us.

One final thought on this subject. Mission, loyalty, and community are easy buzzwords. Enron talked about integrity. Leaders are fond of saying "I've got your back," and those who do are often the first to shove you under a bus. Saying those things and meaning them are different. If you say them and you don't mean them, you're a liar at best and a traitor at worst, sins that are respectively damned to the eighth and ninth circles of hell.[325] And you won't fool anyone.

Limit power and control

> *When I stepped ashore in the United States, I discovered*
> *with amazement to what extent merit was common among*
> *the governed but rare among the rulers.*[326]

Tocqueville's sarcastic comment on the quality of American government may seem particularly apropos right now. But there is something universal about the idea that those who most seek power may be those least suited to having it. Indeed, Tocqueville believed that in some ways leaders in an aristocratic system were superior because power was inherited (and thus at worst distributed more or less by chance, or at best given to those who had been taught to use it) rather than going to those who fought and clawed for it (who might be particularly dangerous when holding it). On balance, though, he saw a benefit in democracy because of the shared interests between the governing and the governed:

---

[324] See for example Al-Gharbi, Musa, "How to Understand the Well-Being Gap between Liberals and Conservatives,"
American Affairs Journal, March 21, 2023; and Feng, Lily, Sara Suzuki, Alberto Medina, SJ McGeady, "Community Connections Matter for the Mental Health of Politically Active Youth," *Tufts Center for Information & Research on Civic Learning and Engagement*, April 27, 2023.
[325] Alighieri, *The Divine Comedy*, "Inferno."
[326] De Tocqueville, *Democracy in America*, "Government by Democracy in America."

In the United States, those responsible for public affairs are often inferior in capability and in moral standards to those men aristocracy would bring to power, but their interests are mingled and identified with those of the majority of their fellow citizens.[327]

That shared interest makes sense as long as those who govern don't succeed in creating too much distance between themselves and the governed. Hirschman notes that leaders will try to do precisely that: "As has already been mentioned, the short-run interest of management is to increase its own freedom of movement."[328] That's true whether "management" is the leadership of a company or the politicians in power. They want to stay there, and they want to control as much as they can. That is a natural result of humans' drive for status, which is inherent in all primates. The most extreme examples are historical:

The well-known Egyptian effort to master death is matched in the first chapter of Exodus by a new Egyptian effort to master birth. Taken together, they represent the core of the human effort to resist change and decay through technology and magic, as well as the tyrant's wish both to be his own source and to live forever.[329]

Most modern leaders don't aspire to quite the same level of absolute control over life and death as Pharaoh, although Vladimir Putin, Kim Jong Un, and some tech CEOs might come close. Some of the modern ideas of transhumanism (artificial extension of human existence)[330] are more than a little scary, especially considering the kinds of people who would probably wind up becoming transhuman.

---

[327] Ibid, "What Are the Real Advantages Derived by American Society from Democratic Government."

[328] Hirschman, *Exit, Voice, and Loyalty,* "The Elusive Optimal Mix of Exit and Voice."

[329] Kass, *Founding God's Nation,* "Into the House of Bondage."

[330] "Transhumainsm," Wikimedia Foundation, last modified January 20, 2025, **https://en.wikipedia.org/wiki/Transhumanism.**

From a leadership standpoint, the challenge for any organization (again, whether political, religious, or economic) is to limit the amount of power so that those in authority can serve the legitimate needs of their constituents, but no more. Asymmetries must exist in any complex society, but the point is for them to be mutually beneficial rather than exploitative:

> *Authority ranking relationships are based on a model of asymmetry among people who are linearly ordered along some hierarchical social dimension... People higher in rank have prestige, prerogatives, and privileges that their inferiors lack, but subordinates are often entitled to protection and pastoral care.*[331]

The ideal is servant leadership, as articulated most fully by Robert Greenleaf:

> *The servant-leader is servant first... It begins with the natural feeling that one wants to serve, to serve first. Then conscious choice brings one to aspire to lead. That person is sharply different from one who is leader first, perhaps because of the need to assuage an unusual power drive or to acquire material possessions...*[332]

That idea, of course, is expressed in the Bible: "Rather, let the greatest among you be as the youngest, and the leader as the servant."[333]

The problem is that servant leadership is another one of those things, like mission, that's easy to say but doesn't necessarily get done in practice. All kinds of politicians who are very fond of their perks and privileges call themselves "public servants" even if they don't usually seem to be doing much to serve the public. The more power the individual accrues, the more likely they are to be corrupted by it; also, the more power goes with the position, the more likely it is to attract the wrong kind of leader. So expressing the ideals of servant leadership is useful, but almost certainly not sufficient without structural safeguards.

---

[331] Fiske, Alan, "The Four Elementary Forms of Sociality: Framework for a Unified Theory of Social Relations," *Psychological Review 99(4)*, 1992.
[332] **https://www.greenleaf.org/what-is-servant-leadership/**, excerpted from *The Servant as Leader* by Robert Greenleaf, 1970.
[333] Luke 22:26.

Explicitly limiting the role of leaders to precisely defined domains where they can serve the interests of the followers doesn't just promote individual autonomy; it can help mitigate that risk of corruption, selfishness, and jealousy. A smaller scope of control helps prevent a particular leader from acquiring too much power, prestige, and insulation from those that are led. The Catholic principle of subsidiarity explicitly tries to limit the domains where power is exercised as much as possible. Tocqueville found a particular benefit in the fact that historically American institutions developed power from the bottom up rather than the top down, keeping control at the local level:

> *The individual township was the place where local interests, passions, duties, and rights clung together and it fostered at its heart real political activity which was active, thoroughly democratic, and republican.*[334]

That decentralization conferred many benefits. It avoided concentrations of power in a single tyrant or governing junta; it gave people a participatory stake in deliberations and outcomes; and it made leaders more agile and responsive to immediate needs.

A smaller scope of control imposes friction on the ability of a business genius or a wise philosopher king to make positive changes. Steve Jobs had initially invited former SEC chairman Arthur Levitt to sit on Apple's board, "But then Jobs read a speech Levitt had given about corporate governance, which argued that boards should play a strong and independent role, and he telephoned to withdraw the invitation."[335] Maybe Apple benefited from a board that didn't limit Jobs' genius – the history of its stock price after Jobs' return would suggest that was true. But in most cases, unchecked control in a government or a company just creates tyranny. There's a reason the U.S. government has separation of powers, not just at the federal level (executive, legislative, and judiciary) but between the federal and state governments.

---

[334] De Tocqueville, *Democracy in America*, "On the Origins of the Anglo-Americans and on its Importance for their Future."
[335] Isaacson, *Steve Jobs*, "The Restoration: The Loser Now Will be Later to Win."

As electronic monitoring and artificial intelligence begin to give leaders even more means of unchecked control, it becomes increasingly important to impose systemic constraints. A selfish human in power, aided and abetted by amoral algorithms, opens up unpleasant new vistas. Kearns and Roth describe states in game theory where in a "selfish equilibrium," everyone is worse off. Selfishly maximizing individual outcomes at the expense of the group is the most famous and obvious of those. A "winner take all" system designed to award massive power to whoever claws their way to the top seems like a prime candidate for just that kind of dysfunction.

> *When equilibrium is described as a selfish standoff, it's not particularly surprising that sometimes equilibrium can be undesirable to any particular individual in the system... or even to the entire population.[336]*

Accrual of power for its own sake is simply bad for society and individuals – even those who are powerful.

Make compliance easy and incentivized

Sandel has a particular distaste for the word "incentivize." It can imply that we're trying to monetize doing the right thing, which can corrupt the intention behind doing it:

> *It points to the degrading effect of market valuation and exchange on certain goods and practices... It is a mistake to assume that incentives are additive... The intrusion of market norms crowded out their sense of civic duty.[337]*

Bazerman concurs:

> *But the primary danger of compliance systems lies in their contortion of the decision-making process. Suddenly, instead of thinking about doing the right thing, employees focus on calculating the costs and benefits of compliance versus noncompliance – and about trying to outsmart the system.[338]*

---

[336] Kearns and Roth, *The Ethical Algorithm*, "Jump Balls and Bombs."
[337] Sandel, *What Money Can't Buy*, "How Markets Crowd Out Morals."
[338] Bazerman and Tenbrunsel, *Blind Spots*, "Placing False Hope in the 'Ethical Organization.'"

Brennan observes the same, referring to a "motivational crowding effect."[339] I agree that compliance in a mission-driven organization can and should be intrinsic, not extrinsic. Indeed, even being able to think about "can versus should" is a positive sign. Returning to the artificial intelligence example above, a mission-driven organization should carefully contemplate not just whether an algorithm can perform a task, but also whether that is a good task for an algorithm to perform and whether it may have unintended consequences.

However, having run several compliance organizations, I'm reluctant to conclude that "virtue is its own reward" is a winning motivational strategy. If we want good behavior, it does in fact need to be incentivized, by which I mean that it needs to be easy to comply from both a process and reward perspective. Systems and processes must not make it difficult to do the right thing while also doing what gets you paid. Bazerman seems to agree, noting that "Leaders should inventory the informal systems that exist and work to understand the underlying pressures that are put on employees."[340]

If those economic pressures conflict with the formal compliance requirements, the formal compliance requirements will probably lose. They will especially tend to lose in "should" scenarios – people will likely obey strictly defined "can" rules about not committing illegal acts, but in gray areas the informal "rules that matter" will win over the formal values statements that don't. The Alcoa example that Brennan cites is useful. People need to actually be rewarded for doing things that align with the organization's values as they were under Paul O'Neill. I would further guess that Alcoa likely went to great lengths to make it easier to operate safely, rather than merely providing lip service to the idea.

Richard Kyte draws a critical distinction between ethics, which are embedded in the mission and culture, and compliance, which is following an explicit set of rules.

---

[339] Brennan, English, Hasnas, and Jaworski, *Business Ethics for Better Behavior*, "Psychological Factors: Meaning and Motivation."
[340] Bazerman and Tenbrunsel, *Blind Spots*, "Placing False Hope in the 'Ethical Organization.'"

This reveals a fundamental fact about ethical decision making in the workplace: it is fully effective only within the context of an already established ethical culture. In the absence of such a culture, ethical decision making is severely limited, because the open dialogue upon which it depends cannot take place.... Codes, policies, and sanctions, after all, are just tools. In the right hands, they can be used positively and effectively. In the wrong hands, they can be destructive.[341]

Seth Godin states it simply as, "Culture defeats tactics every time, which is why strategy is often about creating culture."[342]

Compliance needs to serve the organization's mission. And making it easy to comply does not mean erecting fortresses of bureaucracy. In fact, Jesus explicitly warned:

Woe also to you scholars of the law! You impose on people burdens hard to carry, but you yourselves do not lift one finger to touch them.[343]

Yes, there need to be standards, and a large organization will need mechanisms to enforce those standards. When those mechanisms are transparent, helpful, and aligned with the organization's values, they serve the valuable function of an immune system protecting against attacks on the organization's integrity. But if the mechanisms metastasize into self-serving, self-protecting, self-perpetuating bureaucracy, they do more harm than good. The same is true if compliance is enforced through terror, which we saw in Chapter Three will actually make it harder for people to do the right thing by keeping them in a state of cognitive distress.

Making it easy to comply is important regardless of whether you view altruism as a finite resource that can be depleted or as a muscle that grows through exercise. Sandel posits two possible views of people's "reservoirs" of altruistic behavior. Either:

---

[341] Kyte, *Ethical Business*, Introduction.
[342] Godin, Seth, *This Is Strategy* (Authors Equity, 2024), #76.
[343] Luke 11:46.

> *Reckless expenditures of altruism in social and economic life
> not only deplete the supply available for other public
> purposes. They even reduce the amount we have left for our
> families and friends...*

Or...

> *Altruism, generosity, solidarity, and civic spirit are not like
> commodities that are depleted with use. They are more like
> muscles that develop and grow stronger with exercise. One
> of the defects of a market-driven society is that it lets these
> virtues languish. To renew our public life we need to
> exercise them more strenuously.[344]*

The first hypothesis is closer to Bazerman's idea of a "moral equilibrium," while the second is closer to Ariely's view that good and bad behaviors unconsciously reinforce themselves. Sandel himself favors the second hypothesis.

I have sympathy for both views even though they're contradictory on their face. While I've observed some "moral balancing" behavior in myself, I've also found that indulging in a vice lowers my threshold to indulge in it again. For our purposes here, the answer doesn't matter. Whichever is true, or whether each one is true under specific circumstances, the best approach is to make it easier for people to comply. If that's accomplished, then people can easily exercise their "compliance muscle," while not drawing down from a potentially limited reservoir of altruism.

---

[344] Sandel, *What Money Can't Buy*, "How Markets Crowd Out Morals."

For example, Bazerman criticizes the auditing profession at some length for systemic flaws that he characterizes as corrupting the profession. He asserts that "the current U.S. audit system makes it 'psychologically impossible,' because of motivated blindness, for even the most honest auditors to make objective judgments."[345] That statement seems to me to go a little far. In my decades of experience with auditors, most of them go to heroic lengths to maintain professional skepticism in the face of client pressure. But it would undoubtedly be easier for them if a viable alternative incentive structure were somehow created that didn't require such heroic efforts. Robert Conway, an audit partner before his time at the Public Company Accounting Oversight Board, observed that:

> It is unfortunately easy to lose sight of this higher duty [to investors] in the day-to-day execution of the audit. On [a] daily basis, the auditor is focused on delivering a high level of "client service." This means being timely and professional while also trying to minimize disruption to the client's daily operations… The last thing the auditor wants to do is to upset the client.[346]

As I noted in the first chapter, even my own views as the "most auditor-like auditor" shifted when I began performing due diligence and the subject of my work became the target rather than the client. Incentives matter.

~~~

In the end, the way forward to doing the right thing will be a constant battle. There will be no simple solution. In part, that's because innovating against entrenched systems of power is hard. Machiavelli notes:

> And it ought to be remembered that there is nothing more difficult to take in hand, more perilous to conduct, or more uncertain in its success, than to take the lead in the introduction of a new order of things, because the innovator has for enemies all who have done well under the old conditions, and lukewarm defenders in those who may do well under the new.[347]

---

[345] Bazerman and Tenbrunsel, *Blind Spots*, "Why We Fail to Fix Our Corrupted Institutions."
[346] Conway, *The Truth About Public Accounting*, "Deciphering Conflicting Signals."
[347] Machiavelli, *The Prince*, Ch. VI.

That is not necessarily a bad thing. Traditions matter. There is something to the idea that a system that has withstood the test of time must have something positive going for it. We need to avoid the tendency to catastrophize, to pretend that things are uniquely bad at this moment in history, to imagine golden ages that have gone before or to come, to believe that everything is so much worse now. Reading Machiavelli, Ibn Khaldun, Juvenal, Thucydides, or the Bible should disabuse us of the idea that things were somehow marvelous before they were corrupted by our current generation, market economy, or leaders. As we work for reform, we must be careful not to be "the idiot who praises with enthusiastic tone all centuries but this and every country but his own."[348] That is itself a form of selfishness and ingratitude.

The challenge is to preserve the good while improving the bad.

I've suggested that improvement be approached with humility, a sense of mission, limits on any individual's scope of control, and an understanding of incentives. Easy to say. And yet each of those recommendations carries the seeds of its own corruption. Alinsky says, "In the world as it is, the solution of each problem inevitably creates a new one."[349] Creating an organization with a strong sense of mission risks developing discriminatory in-groups and out-groups. Incentives, no matter how well crafted, can be gamed. Hirschman pessimistically observes that "each recovery mechanism is itself subject to the forces of decay which have been invoked here all along."[350]

Tocqueville noted that, "American legislators display but little trust in human integrity, while assuming always that men are intelligent."[351] Unfortunately, intelligent people who lack integrity can be counted on not just to behave badly, but to do so in clever ways.

---

[348] Gilbert, W.S. and Arthur Sullivan, *The Mikado*, 1885, "As Some Day It May Happen."
[349] Alinsky, *Rules for Radicals*, "The Purpose."
[350] Hirschman, *Exit, Voice, and Loyalty*, "The Elusive Optimal Mix of Exit and Voice."
[351] De Tocqueville, *Democracy in America*, "The Necessity of Examining What Happens in Individual States Before Considering the Union as a Whole."

It would be wonderful if everyone subscribed to the Swedish concept of "lagom," the idea of having just the right amount – everything in moderation.[352] It would be wonderful, but that would require people to stop being selfish, jealous, shortsighted, stubborn, and ungrateful. Sometimes lost in the story of the Acts of the Apostles, who "had everything in common,"[353] was the fact that their sense of community resulted directly from them all being "filled with the Holy Spirit."[354] Barring a miracle,[355] humans don't tend to behave that way. As Walter Ciszek noted even of the Church that he loved enough to endure twenty years of confinement for its sake:

> *The Church is full of human failings because it is composed of human beings; it has its share of scandals and bad leaders, of mediocre minds, of selfishness and skin-deep spirituality, of fallible and imperfect men who do not always practice what they preach.[356]*

Even organizations explicitly dedicated to the spiritual betterment of the human soul are subject to human frailty. It's hardly realistic to think that organizations dedicated to making money or exercising political control are going to be free of it. Thomas Sowell, as a believer in the "constrained vision" of human behavior, said:

> *Implicit in the unconstrained vision is the notion that the potential is very different from the actual, and that means exist to improve human nature toward its potential, or that such means can be evolved or discovered, so that man will do the right thing for the right reason, rather than for the ulterior psychic or economic rewards.[357]*

---

[352]"Lagom," Wikimedia Foundation, last modified September 1, 2024, **https://en.wikipedia.org/wiki/Lagom**.
[353] Acts 5:32.
[354] Acts 5:31.
[355] And as Ibn Khaldun observes, "Miracles cannot be used as analogies for ordinary affairs and constitute no argument against them." (Ibn Khaldun, *The Muqaddimah*, Ch.3.)
[356] Ciszek, *He Leadeth Me*, "Faith."
[357] Sowell, *A Conflict of Visions*, "Trade-Offs Versus Solutions."

Although Sowell and Alinsky represent opposite political tendencies, they both agree with Father Ciszek that this "unconstrained vision" simply does not reflect human reality. Alinsky's views on political realism and power politics align quite well with Sowell's constrained vision. "It is painful to accept fully the simple fact that one begins from where one is, that one must break free of the web of illusions one spins about life."[358]

We won't change human nature. Saint Anthony the Great said, "One should not say that it is impossible to reach a virtuous life; but one should say that it is not easy. Nor do those who have reached it find it easy to maintain."[359] We can, however, better align structures and incentives. And we can recognize that the struggle for improvement is a necessary and inevitable part of our development, as individuals and as a society. Indeed, the Dalai Lama highlights the very obstacles we face, very much including human opposition, as necessary to our spiritual growth.[360] We can try within our organizations, and perhaps more importantly within ourselves, to battle against our natural tendency to be selfish, jealous, shortsighted, stubborn, and ungrateful. "Because if the soul isn't tempted, exercised, and tried by struggles and temptations, its sense of wisdom cannot awaken."[361]

The point of those trials must be to awaken our humility. To remind us that we are at our best when we serve a mission beyond our own selfish desires. To teach us that the world is never under our control – nor should we want it to be. To help us understand our own frailties and those of the people around us.

---

[358] Alinsky, *Rules for Radicals*, "The Purpose."

[359] This attribution is a bit suspect, as I can find no source for it, nor can I find the quote in *The Sayings of the Holy Desert Fathers* by Saint Palladius (Wallis Budge translation) or *The Life of Anthony* by Athanasius of Alexandria (Old Book New translation).

[360] HH Dalai Lama and Cutler, *The Art of Happiness*, "Shifting Perspective."

[361] San Juan de la Cruz, *Noche Oscura del Alma*, Book 1 Ch.14. My translation.

In a recent homily, one of our local priests noted that in Jesus' healing of the paralytic in Mark 2:1-12, he told the man to pick up the mat he had lain on and take it with him. Not leave it behind, but carry it with him.[362] And indeed, the same instruction to carry the mat is found in the healings in Luke 5:17-26, Matthew 9:1-7, and John 5:1-11. The priest observed that even when we are healed, we still carry our mats – the wounds and scars of our interior brokenness with us. And that's okay. We aren't perfect. But by struggling against our temptations, we can be better.

The year 2025 is a Jubilee Year of Hope in the Catholic Church. Whatever our religious or ethical traditions, perhaps we can hopefully, and also realistically, find our way forward.

---

[362] Father Frank Fano, homily at Our Lady of Mt. Carmel Roman Catholic Church of Ridgewood, NJ, January 17, 2025.

Acknowledgments

First and most important, to my wife, Veronica – any spiritual progress I've made is because God put you in my life. And of course my eternal gratitude to my parents, Erica and Malcolm McClure, who instilled in me a love of learning and the importance of *menschlichkeit*.[363]

Many thanks to Ken Brownfield, Don Charles, Gabriel McClure, Richard McClure, Will Lukang, Jim Towey, and Micah Yairi, who provided valuable insights in the early drafting. Sunil Kuchroo and Tom Conner have been essential contributors to both the theory and practice of doing the right thing.

Dr. Jason Brennan, Dr. Carole Sargent, and Dr. Quentin Dupont, S.J., all of Georgetown University, were very generous with their time and support, particularly on the nuances of publishing.

I also owe an incalculable debt to the spiritual guides in my life, especially the religious communities of Our Lady of Mount Carmel in Ridgewood, NJ and St. Augustine's Roman Catholic Church in Newark, NJ, as well as the East Region of the Missionaries of Charity.

I have benefited tremendously over the years from the wisdom and support of too many professional mentors and colleagues to mention individually. You know who you are. Thank you. The Dalai Lama further tells us that our enemies, those who maliciously cause us harm, are also great teachers to be revered for giving us the opportunity to practice patience.[364] There are far, far fewer of those in my life. You know who you are too. Thank you.

---

[363] There's no good translation from the Yiddish, but there's a good definition here: https://jewishjournal.com/judaism/359493/the-nobel-prize-for-menschlichkeit/

[364] HH Dalai Lama and Cutler, *The Art of Happiness*, "Shifting Perspective."

It's been pointed out to me by gracious readers whom I greatly respect that this book is heavy on the negative and light on the positive. I've made a few editorial changes to reflect that feedback, but the tone remains on the darker side. Let me be clear – I believe there is a tremendous amount of grace and love in the human experience. I see it every day with my family, people in my church, and people I work with. And I believe that striving for improvement, by reason and by faith, in ourselves and in our organizations, is absolutely a necessary and fruitful endeavor. Why then so much focus in this book on the bad rather than the good? In part because it's easier to identify problems than solutions, as I mentioned in my opening note to the reader. But also because identifying those problems is the essential key to identifying the *need* for solutions. To misquote Albert Einstein, "If I had an hour to solve a problem I'd spend 55 minutes thinking about the problem and 5 minutes thinking about solutions."[365] A great many traditions, religious and otherwise, set out solutions to the problems of human selfishness, jealousy, shortsightedness, stubbornness, and ingratitude, but as the popular saying goes, "admitting you have a problem is the first step in recovery." I have to keep reminding myself daily that I have a problem. To all those who help me see that and overcome it, again, thank you.

Notes on notes

I've used a modified version of the Chicago Style for footnotes; since most books these days (certainly in my library) seem to be electronic, I have provided chapter references rather than page numbers.

---

[365] Apparently not a real Einstein quote, according to
https://quoteinvestigator.com/2014/05/22/solve/

Forthcoming books by the author

Accounting for Trust

We live in a world of declining trust. What if there were someone whose job was to tell the truth? Oh wait, there is. Exploring the unique role of the CPA and the auditing profession in enhancing trust in society.

Where the Algorithms Lie (with Will Lukang)

We run the risk that technology may corrupt us because we're corruptible, and that it may manipulate us because we're manipulable. A framework for assessing the responsible development and deployment of algorithms in a world of human frailty.